Carillon

of
God, Lord Jesus & An Angel

Carillon

of
God, Lord Jesus & An Angel

Mysteries of Contact
Heavenly Hearts Are Real

Not
Near-Death Experience

Snowye
Pacific Northwest, USA

979-8-88615-102-2 (Paperback)
979-8-88615-103-9 (Hardback)
979-8-88615-104-6 (Ebook)

Credit & Attribution

The Light Within 1723 KJV Holy Bible
Photograph: Arlen Fletcher

KJV Bible Verse Quotations:John Baskett, Thomas Newcomb, Henry Hills, The Bible Containing the Old Testament and The New: Newly Translated out of the Original Tongues, Translations Diligently Compared and Revised (London: John Baskett Printer to His Majesty, 1723)

Formation Flight
Photograph F–22 Raptors: Air Force Staff Sgt. James Richardson
The appearance of U.S. Department of Defense (DoD) visual information does not imply or constitute DoD endorsement.

Chaos at the Heart of Orion (cover and inside pages)
https://www.nasa.gov/multimedia/imagegallery/image_feature_693.html
Image credit: *NASA/JPL–Caltech/STScI*

Small Gold Ribbon #Ba (indexes headings)
https://pixabay.com/vectors/gold–ribbon–ribbon–heraldry–design–1477305/
AlLes: https://pixabay.com/users/alles–2597842/

Horizontal Bar Flourish
Attribution: <a href="https://www.freepik.com/vectors/wedding–line">
Wedding line vector created by starline–www.freepik.com</a>

Free–Flying Dove (cover) iStock.com Image 121337476 Credit: Irochka_T

Old Lavender Scroll iStock.com Image 92496870 Credit: JimLarkin

Old Red Scroll iStock.com Image 139384781 Credit: JimLarkin

Free Flying Dove: Lotus_studio/Shutterstock.com Stock Photo ID: 41437675

White Pigeon: Macrovector/Shutterstock.com Stock Vector ID: 1132590464

Flying Dove Lotus_studio/Shutterstock.com Stock Photo ID: 43753009

Feathers Gluiki/Shutterstock.com Stock Vector ID: 1084926038

White Dove LittlePrefectStock/Shutterstock.com Stock Photo ID: 454003444

Flying Dove Duda Vasailii/Shutterstock.com Stock Vector ID: 195656804

Black Box https://www.shutterstock.com/image-vector/vector-silver-glowing-light-glitter-background-526104514

Flourish www.iStock.com Vector: 888852920 Credit: Misao NOYA

Ellen G. White Quotations
Public Domain and Special Permissions

Wonderful Team: Ryan, James, Nadine and Jess at Inks and Bindings

Dedication

Son of God and Son of Man
It took my eyes and the ability to see to accomplish writing Carillon. I thank thee, dear Savior, Lord of Angels, Commander of Heaven, Jesus Christ. Miraculous healings and sending the Holy Spirit Comforter to strengthen and minister to me made Carillon possible. Thou art my Chosen One. Eternally I worship how great thou art. Thank you for Creation and for Life.

Precious Beloved Husband
My most precious one, Zach, who obliged as proofreader and editor, was instrumental in creating this work. Zach is the quantum of my world. He provided encouragement. Zach is a precious gift from God. I am thankful for him every day. His prayers are heard—and answered. On my way toward the pew for the first time with Zach, Jesus joyfully told me two times, "Marry him." Angel Daniel was assisting, wings filling the sanctuary. A few hours later, surprising me after Church, Zach jubilantly proposed.

Memorable
I am eternally grateful to my late husband, Alan. God gifted this incredible Abraham's Child as a healer and seer of the future.
He gave me solace.

Treasured
Angel Daniel's oath of loyalty and loving care are precious. He watches over every detail of my life with enthusiasm. His ministry on all levels of my being with his love and strengthening seems without end.

Honored
Our parents are now departed and held dearly with grandparents and our ancestors. I look forward to a magnificent celebration with them all on that Great Day. It's the quintessential beginning of a new life to see our departed son, meet Zach's parents and eternally rejoice with everyone in the earth made new.

Contents

Preface

Wondering about what a mission should be, besides following the Ten Commandments, was my main pursuit after experiencing Jesus' glorious presence. It was such a privileged and humbling connection; it seemed there should be a meaningful reason. Five years later, it became clear to write *Carillon*. Discernment revealed the title began with C. Searching on the computer, I discovered what seemed to be every C-word possible. Despite help with the probe, I momentarily gave up the enormous vocabulary lesson in C.

A few minutes later, after renewing my search, it was on the computer screen. It will be a worthwhile endeavor should even one person benefit from reading *Carillon*. I'm hoping it's you! Our Father, Jesus, Holy Spirit, angels, and heaven are authentic and genuine. Jesus and the fulfilling Christian experience born in Him are for everyone's benefit. All that's needed is asking with sincerity and Jesus will graciously provide what we yearn for in the depth of our souls.

Holding off from joining a church was on purpose, but I accomplished the venture right on time. The goal was to find a church to meet fellow followers of Jesus Christ. I wanted to attend a church for the rest of my life, experiencing worship, service, and fellowshipping toward lifelong relationships. Epiphany occurred for me to follow the Ten Commandments entirely by worshiping on the Sabbath (sunset Friday to sunset Saturday), and keeping holy the seventh day as our Father ordained and sanctified at the time of Creation. A church that worshiped on the Sabbath outlined in the fourth commandment was indispensable for me in commemorating Creation and obeying God's law.

The desirable place turned out to be a small country church with stately pine trees. Deer and birds were abundant in other wildlife that included bears. It was a charming, traditional church with a membership sharing ideas in tenets of faith along with a healthful diet and lifestyle.

Bible study classes were proceeding quickly. Insightful courses in learning about the Bible were necessary for this book's writing. I knew very little about the Bible and Christianity before because I was never even Christian. Jesus' glorious appearing to me in open vision made it vital to become Christian and central to obey our Father's summary of His eternal law. The Ten Commandments are essential to me because they summarize God's law and represent His righteous character, complete in mercy and grace. Bible instruction led to meaningful enlightenment. The Sanctuary message, Three Angels' Messages, Daniel and Revelation, truth, timelines, type, and antitype in the Bible was gratifying cultivation for me, a serious seeker of Truth. It was just the tip of an ongoing study that will continue throughout eternity alongside the angels in heaven. Since this will be our theme throughout eternity, I felt the importance not to wait until reaching or not reaching heaven, but to learn the grand plan of redemption now.

The Bible wondrously and beautifully defines itself. There is no theology in the Sabbath school teachings that is not contained in and validated by the Bible. The Bible is extensive in mystery, with historical prophecies that have come true and prophesies yet to become fulfilled.

I look forward to daily Bible studies with my husband Zach (I remarried as my previous husband Alan expired). They're on bountiful topics, lending to my much–needed growth and understanding.

Intricate prophetic timelines in the Bible's books of Daniel and Revelation are accurate with confirmation. The facts show proof that prophecy in the Bible comes true. Educated readers cannot deny this primarily based on Bible and Bible–only perusal. Our Father is on time to the day and the hour. The wisdom in the Bible provides unquestionable evidence and examples for successful life guidelines, making correct life choices, along with the correct path to spending eternity in heaven.

Impact through the teachings of the Bible has been profound for me, with significance and understanding provided through open visions. Credibility for the details provided in these open visions came to light with meaningful validation from reading the Holy Bible. However, I needed fundamental life understanding besides biblical tutoring for the desired growth in even understanding I should strive for a Christ–like nature.

Preface

Five years passed after being in an open vision with Jesus until I could rely on my perceptions in communications with heavenly beings. Communications revealed fundamental ideas for my spiritual growth through the sophisticated work of Lord Jesus, the Holy Spirit, and Angel Daniel, which led to writing *Carillon*. I plan ensuing books because there are many more incredible incidents with heavenly hearts to impart.

Snowye
Pacific Northwest, USA
April 30, 2022

Introduction

Communication with heavenly beings—Father, Jesus, the Holy Spirit, and angels—differ from how we usually converse with each other. The best explanation is that it is telepathic, and more. The words I heard came with additional and complete understanding provided in seeing and knowing while I heard them spoken. Seeing and knowing came with visualizations, too. The seeing and knowing is an aspect of the communications that I now understand is what Christians call discernment. I know you can hear heavenly presences, too!

The actual spoken words I heard were God's, for all my life, before the glorious experience with our Lord Jesus. Now I enjoy our Father, Jesus, the Holy Spirit, and Angel Daniel's spoken words and messages. God resounds louder than Jesus, the Holy Spirit, and angels. God's voice is enrapturing. I would describe Jesus' voice as distinct, deep, manly, smooth, and resonating. His words are distinctive in that His loving statements were also commanding at the same time. The Holy Spirit provides a euphoric bodily feeling of electrical–type vibrations or energy. The euphoria is physical and elates my entire inner makeup, mental, emotional, and spiritual. Like our conscience, the voice of the Holy Spirit is small. The Holy Spirit can alarm and emphasize, as well. Words heard alarmingly contain visualizations, intense electrical shaking, hum, and a strong physical buzz.

Angels work together, directed by our Father and Jesus with the Holy Spirit, providing incredibly loving strength. Angel Daniel has a sophisticated voice and a different word placement in his sentences. Other angels also have distinct voices, just like we have unique and individual sounds to our voices here on fallen planet earth.

God, Jesus, the Holy Spirit, and Angel Daniel's words and statements are simple and short. These succinct statements are the actual words heard. Relaying of details and fine points of all that heavenly hearts communicated to me with these spoken words and open visions are a tremendous pleasure. The additional explanations are from what discernment provided. A minor example is what Angel Daniel asked other angels who had gathered in an angels' forum. Somehow, I was allowed, and given permission, to experience what Angel Daniel was asking the other angels to help investigate,

Angel Daniel: What marks my girl?

Seeing and hearing him say the above brought an incredible feeling of connection, fondness, intimacy, and loving affection. It was Daniel's reference—*my girl*. It was precious to hear this heartening reference because it is the same way I lovingly referred to him—*my angel*. Discernment revealed that he was asking what favorable seals I contained (entire lifetime) to abide in heaven? I do not know if there were any acceptable marks because the experience ended with the captivating question. Hopefully, there were notable marks and seals toward my living in heaven.

Quotes are something I simply adore. Please be happy to find many that truly help describe and pertain. After the open vision with Lord Jesus, it was incredible that things I did not know actually were accurate, resulting in the quotes provided. Most of the selections are from the Bible, and the Spirit of Prophecy works of Ellen G. White.

Biblical quotes in *Carillon* replace the old English letter called a medial S with our modern version letter S. Old English medial S resembles a modern lowercase f.

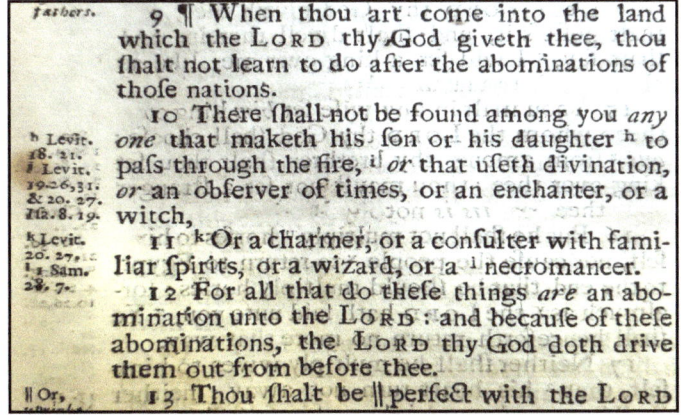

Page from author's 1723 KJV Bible

(Deuteronomy 18:9–12)

xvii

The original 1611 King James Version contained the Apocrypha, which was removed in 1885. I used this 1723 King James Version because it contains the Apocrypha with its references, plus it was after the printers and editors fixed most of the typos from 1611.

Photo: Arlen Fletcher
The Light Within (Author's 1723 KJV)

Is there anything more I can do for you?
Can I see God's face too?

Carillon of God

Our All-Seeing Protector

As a young 17–year–old teenage girl contemplating life ahead, I sometimes wondered and asked God if anyone would ever want to marry me. Speculation was on what my future husband's personality and looks might be like. Uplifted by the Holy Spirit, our Righteous Father brought an open vision of marital love and happiness for my future. Kneeling on the bed and looking out the window, there was the sight of my future husband, Alan. I saw him through a paned glass window, and he was laughing his rolling and hearty laugh. I felt intense and elating love, simultaneously with an exhilarating spirit in discerning how our marriage would be. God was giving me an open vision of a delightful, fulfilling marriage and love. Thrilled with what I was seeing, I asked our Father,

Snowye: Dear God, what is his name!
Our Father: His name is Alan.

Snowye:	Where does he live?
Our Father:	In Vermont.
Snowye:	Okay. This is very fine and what I would like. I'll go there now and see him!
Our Father:	No, not now.
Snowye:	But what if he's not there later, and what if he finds someone in the meantime? I'm sure that I'm going so we can get married.
Our Father:	Do not worry. He will be there all his life.
Snowye:	Oh. But then, why not now? If he is going to be my husband…
Our Father:	Not until later.

I accepted all that my much–loved Father said. The hope, wish, and goal were for a traditional family like Dad and Mom, married with all seven of us children who were their own. Despite writing Alan's name, I forgot the conversation with our Father and Alan's name in the distractions and bustle of a young girl's life.

Do Not Touch the Water

Getting up in the usual routine, I put on coffee to brew while showering. Before the internet and cell phones era, communication with friends and family was in person, by regular postal snail mail, or with a landline telephone call. There used to be many telephone booths in buildings and on the streets for a quarter's convenience. While taking the coffeepot in hand, I heard our Father speaking a warning,

Our Father: Do not touch the water.

Snowye: I'm just now getting coffee.

Our Father: Do not touch the water. Do not drink it;
              do not use it for anything. It is poison.

Snowye: Thank you for telling me.

I saw in a short open vision the water coming from the spout. My old–fashioned 1911 kitchen sink was streaming tainted, milky-colored water. I had to warn everyone right away. The first thing to do was to call Mom. I knew she would get the word to the rest of the family and friends. I told Mom not to use the poisoned water. It was difficult to relay how I knew it, but she understood when I explained it to her. Namely, that it was just heard when I turned the water on. My mother was thankful because she was getting ready to drink a cup of freshly brewed coffee already poured and in her hand. I was grateful for the excellent timing Father provided. We could alert friends and neighbors. It didn't matter what they thought about God's warning to save lives and escape sickness's anguish. Anyone who paid attention avoided toxic, cancer–causing water.

A few hours later, Mom called. She told me to turn on the television. Warnings were all over the news channels not to use the tainted water with newscasters saying the tap water had become poisoned. A manufacturing company had accidentally dumped gigantic amounts of PCBs (polychlorinated biphenyls or pentachlorobiphenyl) into the river water. The usually clear, snowmelt river water was the city water supply. We know PCBs to be sure cancer–causing chemical substances.

From that point on, I did not trust city water supplies. I obtained distilled bottled water for all drinking and cooking.

Many decades passed using steam distilled bottled water. Drinking distilled water turned out to be fortunate because I didn't get any fluoride in my system. I have read that fluoride collects in the pineal gland, obstructing and hampering our divine connection with God, The Monarch of the Universe.

Go Now and Hide

I was washing the breakfast dishes when I discerned sinister depravity. A mustard–colored van was cruising the condominium streets where I lived.

The van had just gone by the window. The strange part was that it was moving along too slowly. It was a predatory cruising that raised the hair on the back of my neck. There was curiosity at the same time in wanting to see.

Our Father: Go now and hide. Close all the
drapes. Get away from the windows.
Stay down low. Do not be seen.
Snowye: Yes, my Father.

I saw the washed–out, mustard–colored van again for a moment outside a window when leaving the kitchen. I went into the living room, bending over while walking to avoid being seen through any windows. The van continued creeping with a determined slowness. Years later I can still hear the motor's idling putt–putt in my mind's ear.

I wasn't to be seen and make as if no one were home. I obeyed, ducking low in the living room, with the windows, blinds, and drapes already closed.

There was no peeking, but I listened to them. I did not hear their words. I just heard the voices between a girl and the man in the van, outside, but close to one of the living room windows. She got into the truck after their brief conversation. I heard the door to the van shut. It was alarming because it was then that the van sped off. No more cruising slowly; instead, the driver accomplished his aim. I asked God to please watch over the girl.

It must have been an hour or two later. Again, the television news was informative. There was a shootout a block away in a large empty field with police and a man whose vehicle was the distressed, mustard–colored van. The guilty party held a 14–year–old girl captive during the shootout. The police shot him dead. The girl was unharmed, aside from the emotional trauma she suffered.

This connection with God was one that I never relayed much to other people. I was grateful for being watched over and warned. I didn't wonder why there was a warning to hide because I thought all people communicated this way with our Father during this time of my life. Many years later, in talking about various occurrences, I figured out that most people did not believe in communication with God. I verified this by doing a personal survey over a few years. Should the opportunity present itself, I would randomly ask people if God ever spoke to them.

[8]Keep me as the apple of the eye, hide me under the shadow of thy wings, [9]From the wicked that oppress me, *from* my deadly enemies, *who* compass me about.
(Psalms 17:8, 9)

2

Pliant Harmony

While managing and running a rental property of fifty–six log cabins and duplexes, an event is still cryptic. Ordinarily, I never read the crime page of the newspaper. I looked at it this particular morning, finding an article about a masked and gloved robber who took a 71–year–old lady's jewelry. It was offensive because not only did this masked person take her jewelry, but he held a knife to her throat while doing it. Taking a knife to her was the worst part because he unnecessarily terrorized the helpless elderly lady on top of taking her not so valuable but sentimental jewelry.

I discerned the jewelry was mostly keepsakes given by family and treasures like gold to her. I thought it was a disgusting act with a helpless, frail lady. It was an infuriatingly immoral and shameful thing to do. How could people do such terrible things to others? I vowed never to read the crime section of the newspaper again. There was no description of the newspaper article's thief except that he was not identifiable because of a full–faced, black knit ski mask hiding his face and black gloves that hid his hands.

The burglar was the first one to enter the office that morning. It was just minutes after I put the paper down. Imagine the shock. Discernment revealed it was the thief in the newspaper article I had just read moments before. I also discerned to be careful from our Father and believed that this man was a deplorable lawbreaker and completely untrustworthy.

I called the police when he left the office. Honestly and bluntly, I told the officer this man was the criminal. I disclosed everything, including that I knew with no evidence or reason to know apart from the scanty newspaper article. The location was a rough, cash–only property. I didn't dare to let even the assistant manager see I was calling the police. It would have resulted in retaliation and possibly my afterlife had word gotten around. So instead, I whispered the phone calls to the police from under my desk.

The police couldn't do anything without proof that the man had committed a crime. He was on the property visiting so–called friends that were not his friends. The friends/tenants feared him and wanted him to leave, but they were afraid to tell him and reasonably wanted help from me. The tenants let on to some valuable information. A rental van was being used to live out of by the criminal and his girlfriend. I thought (Holy Spirit) that maybe the rental van wasn't paid for; therefore, considered stolen property. They seemed to hide out by parking in front of the tenants' unit, off regular roads, and not driving anywhere.

I got the license plate number while doing the daily property walk to check for upkeep and maintenance. I could not tell the tenant that working with the police was already taking place.

When they came into the office again, I assured them of a good outcome with no explanation—to their dismay. I'm sure they thought I was peculiar.

Quickly, the swindler had to be caught before he left. I spoke further to the police from under my desk about the rental van and gave the license plate number. Indeed, police records showed they considered it a stolen vehicle because payments were past due. It was an ideal backdrop for the police to check and question the knife–wielding criminal. The police could legally inspect the rental truck's contents as well.

That day the police arrested the thief and his girlfriend where they parked. The police recovered large amounts of stolen jewelry taken from many ladies. Finally, the lengthy crime spree had ended. Law officers found the jewelry from the lady in the newspaper article, too, in that enormous cache of stolen adornments and booty.

Police headquarters called and said a sheriff's commendation was in order for me. For my safety, I received the recognition without ceremony. They told me they captured an evil and dangerous crook. Police were grateful he would be in jail for a long time. They were incredibly thankful for what they said was unusual help for an outlaw's apprehension.

An FBI agent came into the office. We exchanged pleasantries and he let me view his badge. His first words to me were, "How did you know it was him?" When people came into the office, the FBI agent did the most fantastic thing. He simply backed up to the wall, and it was like he had disappeared and was not there. Tenants entering the office never noticed him, although he stood out in looks with a splendidly fitting suit/tie. We waited until people left the office for our conversation to be private. I didn't want to answer and mainly became silent. Who would believe me? Eventually, responding to his professionally trained pressure, I told the FBI agent that I "just knew."

My simple reply pleased him. The FBI agent asked for help in capturing more criminals. He had conviction and believed in people who could discern. I value him for many reasons. This FBI agent is intelligent, meticulous, comprehensive, and dedicated to doing the right thing, among other superior traits.

It was not this humble servant who captured any criminal lawbreakers. The will for the criminal to be arrested, and any credit given for stopping the terrorizing of vulnerable elderly ladies, is because of our entirely merciful and graceful, glorious, caring, and extraordinary—Creator.

Trust and Obey Our Father

Our Father is a merciful and just God, as evidenced throughout the Bible. It amazed me He would care about details like Abraham and Sarah having children. I thought He would have more significant things on His mind than what children were born, who married who, and when. God is God, after all. Why would we question His mercy or justice with His fashioned creations and what He does with His own created earth by His own loving hands?

I have learned that God cares about our lives' minutest details and the heavenly angels record these details in books. The angels' recordings include our children, our spouse, decisions we make, good or bad facial expressions, how we treat others, and what we think and do in the moments that make up our lives.

My exchanges with God were consistently affectionate until one time, my rapport with Him was on the admonishing side. It was difficult and scary to be in love with a man three thousand miles away and daring to meet for the first time. It was much easier for coward me just to run away. I convinced Alan that we should just drop it all. Alan honorably and elegantly agreed to an uncomplicated end to please me. As he told me afterward, there were immediate ramifications for him—lying down on the floor because it felt like a hefty weight of

> ⁷But
>
> Even the very hairs of your head are all numbered. Fear not therefore: ye are of more value than many sparrows.
>
> (Luke 12:7)

bricks piled on top of his chest. The Father told Alan firmly we were to stay together. After telling Alan it was over, I had just gotten off the phone, and we were still friends. I heard a loud voice while thinking about my next steps and goals. It was as if He was yelling at me. Highly displeased, God chastised me. He said it once with an emphatic, low, and loud voice. It was a command and manner comprising complete unhappiness, love, and strength that no one would ever dare question or disobey.

Our Father: You will be with Alan. Or you will regret it all the days of your life!

Snowye: Yes, my God, who I love very much. I will be with Alan. How do I get back together with him?

Our Father: Talk with him next time he calls.

I understood with insight that "all the days of your life!" meant any eternity I might be bound for—not just the physical earthly lifespan. It was flatly plain that He meant what He said. Indeed, it seemed to be the mighty God some people spoke of in the Old Testament. I knew not to dare think of disobeying our omnipotent Father. (Instead, now I think of His law, the Ten Commandments.)

I also trusted that God would help us mend our relationship. As God instructed, I spoke with Alan when he called. I would have talked to Alan under any circumstances. Also, it was now powerfully a part of me not to go against our Father's wishes. Alan called back within minutes. We talked about what happened and quickly picked up and continued as if there were never any thoughts to separate.

God is just what we expect for any good thing. His knowledge is infinite. Any of my ability is restricted. Just like a good parent, out of love, guides and admonishes their children, so does our Father guide and admonish us. It made a powerful impression on me, and my wish to obey our heavenly Father tremendously increased. I *would* have regretted it all my life. One conclusive reason is when I look back on miraculous healings for me that took place through Alan's prayers. Another is the profound intimacy my Father established between Him and me.

> The Word of God is quick and powerful, and sharper than any two-edged sword... and is a discerner of the thoughts and intents of the heart.
> White, Ellen G.
> *Early Writings*, p. 25

Our Father Desires and Cultivates Intimacy

The first interactive online game was called *The Realm*. It has adorable tiny cartoon characters with homes and monster grinding to level up the animated personalities. Alan and I both played the game; however, we did not know each other. Both of us had dropped playing The Realm.

Ten years later, for no particular reason, I signed on to see if any old friends were still playing The Realm. One lady friend met a man from New Zealand while playing. He came to America, took one look, gathered her and the kids, and went back to his New Zealand ranch, where they were married. Amazingly, Alan signed into the game the same day I did, and for the same reason, to see if old friends were still there. We met and played the game together, having fun leveling our characters with a group of mutual friends.

Both Alan and I do not take part in online romantic relationships. We became good friends. I helped him with his family and the emotional plight of putting his mother into a nursing home. We shared many things online. I received the glorious open vision with Jesus in–between these events of meeting Alan online and becoming romantic with him. I was immediately a Christian and a devoted, intense follower after experiencing our beloved Savior.

Alan's and my relationship moved from online interaction to talking on the phone. We became romantic with Alan's confident, romantic pursuit. Reared a Roman Catholic Christian, Alan had left Catholicism and was a devout Protestant by then. His help was a phone's call away should I have a question about God or the Bible. I gained a lot from his explanation and expansion. I was interested in his Christian beliefs. Like so many Christians reared from childhood with Jesus Christ in their lives, they have no idea how much a new Christian does not know.

Alan sent me a lovely Valentine's card and letter in the regular snail mail. By this time, we were in love and Alan had asked me to marry him. I thought it would be an excellent idea to have a romantic Bible quote to read to Alan on the phone as a response and thank you for his Valentine's card. I didn't know with my new Christian affinity that people usually cite a verse and not an entire chapter.

Not familiar with the Bible, I needed help to find a romantic passage. I asked God to help me find the best selection. I closed my eyes while randomly opening my Bible. I knew the quotation would be meaningful and the correct one. Deuteronomy 32 was instrumental and perfect in what occurred. Please understand and forgive my disgrace; there have been a few times when I was contrary when speaking with our Father,

Snowye:	My loving God. This simply is not romantic. I have looked and looked.
Our Father:	It is the passage.
Snowye:	Are you sure? I really wanted something romantic.
Our Father:	It is the one.
Snowye:	Well, I do not know how this could be the one because it is not even about a man and a woman.
Our Father:	Alan will explain it to you.
Snowye:	Yes, my God whom I Love, I will do as You say and recite this passage when Alan calls.

It was a test of patience waiting until Alan phoned, which he did every day. When he called, I first asked him to please listen to the Bible passage. Alan read the scripture along with me in his Bible. Before he could say a word, I asked him to please explain what the selection meant to him. Alan explained it was about the Israelites traveling through the desert for forty years. He told me a little more about why this was so for them. We just kept talking, and I thought no more of it. I was confident the passage's romantic sense would reveal sometime later. I was sure that Alan would be integral in showing the romantic significance. Our Father God's character is not to tell an untruth, ever.

Contemplation about the forty years' sojourn the Israelites undertook remained in our conversation. Curiosity was still there about it. I asked what Alan was doing when he was forty years old. As I listened to Alan's story, I remembered where I was and what I was doing when I was forty years old. I then asked what he was doing forty years ago. Looking at events forty years ago proved to be extraordinarily and pointedly life-changing in my intimacy, affinity, closeness, and fondness with our Father. Realization struck me while still talking on the phone with Alan. The thought was no; it couldn't be. Forty years ago, our Father spoke, showing me Alan with his hearty laugh! It took my breath away. I had not thought of it once in forty years. Holy Spirit was present. Insight revealed it was indeed forty years ago! The realization was true. I carefully counted the years since then, and it was exactly right. Forty years. Unquestionably, it was right to the day! It was impactful and meaningful. Alan knew me well by this time and was just as delighted when I told him how our Father showed him to me in answer to my prayer while wondering if anyone would ever want to marry me. I cried about

God establishing such devoted intimacy with me. God gave Alan to me as a special gift. I felt an exceptional love for our Father when realizing and remembering forty years ago. God directly developed an intimate, meaningful, caring, and personal relationship with me. Perfect and rich, it is as if there is no one else in the world. Cultivated and purposeful, it feels glorious to have the closeness, acceptance, fondness, affection, and ecstasy with the sublime Creator of all, our Father.

Alan indeed explained what the randomly chosen Bible passage meant as our Father said he would. God wants to have a dear, earnest, personal and caring affection with His people. Contact and warm rapport meet His people's spiritual, intellectual, emotional, and physical needs. The Father ultimately cares about and loves all the valiant aspects of His mysterious and phenomenal Creation. God's tender ministry is especially true without exception for all humankind. And look at what blessedly occurred. We were happily married. The blessings abound in more ways than I can express. I hold love and I'm inspired by our Father on an intense and gratifying level. The Father, Jesus, Holy Spirit, and now Angel Daniel are always lovingly held—near as my breath, close as my heartbeat.

> The relations between God and each soul are as distinct and full as though there were not another soul on earth to share His watchcare, not another soul for whom He gave His beloved Son.
> White, Ellen G.
> *Steps to Christ*, p. 100

Carillon of Lord Jesus

Mysterious Details Ahead
of Jesus' Presence

Contemplating intensely about our earth and what was taking place, I realized there was a conflict going on and that it boiled down to a war between good and evil. There is no excuse for one person starving in this modern era. There is also no excuse for war going on with nations. Earth's general atmosphere involves antihumanism, including rampant paedophilia, world religion, world government, adrenochrome harvesting, human sacrifice, transhumanism, and other distinctly evil and satanic categories. Being on our Father's side, fighting the Evil One was the only thing making any sense.

> ## True
>
> Satan possesses a mad will for the indestructible bondage of humanity and the entire earth.
>
> Holy Spirit
> January 26, 2018
> (to Snowye)

The good idea was to shop for Christian churches to join. My thinking was, why reinvent the wheel? Christians know about good and evil, so joining up with them and doing a good part in fixing the world by fighting with the good side and getting rid of sin as much as possible—was my inspiration with untrained Christian thinking. I chose a different Christian church four times on Sunday, attending the service. None felt quite right. One large church was parading figures like scarecrows made of straw and rags on wooden poles down the central middle aisle. I didn't know the purpose of placing them on the altar. When the time came to move, I was determined to find the right church to fight the evil. I made a three–year plan to move away from a city of nightlife, gambling, and crime. Finding a place to settle for the rest of my life and never moving again was the intention. The atmosphere of a large city with its population, unhealthy air, and the emergence of defacing and offensive graffiti added to my longtime desire to move to a smaller community. The chosen area included high altitude, serenity, a shrine, a sparse population, and high mountains with forests of pine trees. After reaching the remote village, the nightly dreams with Jesus began. I was being taught in the dreams through a revered and unique book. It might have been the Bible. The teachings were alone with Jesus and occasionally with a few other students.

We would sit or stand in small circular enclosures outside in a lush garden. High–backed benches carved from solid stone defined the circles on two sides. There was an ornate stone pillar holding the treasured book in the center of the ring. Beyond the two stone benches were delightful gardens spreading far and wide with green foliage and large, colorful flowers. The seats could hold three to four people. Three feet was the distance from the benches to the pillar. The garden surroundings furnished a charmingly cozy and shady spot.

It was an enjoyable occasion for forty nights straight. When I awoke after studying, I could not precisely remember what I had learned the night before. There was a vague realization of the various concepts. But I could not express the events into any specific thought, though I meditated on the previous night's education during the day. I remembered being with Jesus, His love, and the good feelings of accomplishment. Honestly, I took these dreams for granted. It seems Jesus was preparing me.

After the last dream, I realized I had made an agreement with Jesus. It was an authentic and binding pact, essential, but now cryptic to me. Unfortunately, I don't remember what the agreement included as I was not recording my dreams and habits like now. After we reached the secretive agreement, there were no more of the teaching dreams with Jesus.

That night, early in the following day, the roof fell in where I was staying. Things started moving along inexplicably and quickly, with peculiar episodes happening.

A massive blizzard made the national news for this small village, especially for the area. The snow was so heavy that the roof collapsed in just one place—mine. Bed was the warm nook providing any solace during the flurry. There were no lights and no heat because there was no electricity because of a power outage. The roof's beam would have fallen right on my head had I been sitting in the usual chair, reading and using the computer. A hole opened to the night sky and stars after the ceiling caved in. The wooden beam was at an angle so that the computer wasn't hit, but my head would have been. It made a mess with mud, black sludge, roofing material, snow, and wetness all over the floor and everything else in the room. It was a shock and disorienting to look up and see stars in the dark. I went back to bed until morning. They hastened me to another room later that daybreak, and all was fine. Except my friends did not think all was fine. They insisted I go with them and get out of that place. It was difficult because I was being trained as the assistant manager for the property. I lost not only a place to live but gave up a job that went by the wayside, too. There was a camper trailer to live in on my friend's property. Bathing facilities were inside their main house. The owners removed the trailer's heater for repair, but they did not replace it for some unknown reason.

Sitting by the window, at a table with seating cushions that could make into a bed when combined with the table, I prayed to God because I was too cold all the time. The daytime warmth did not offset the chill taken at night. Being frigid was the case, despite a small space heater used in the bed under the covers. You would think it would be hot sleeping like that; however, there was no recovery from the chill. Going physically downhill seemed to be what was happening. The state of affairs made me weaker each day in trying to cope. I thought it might not be possible to survive under the current circumstances. There was no fear in my surmising, just the thought. Also, I reflected that there needed to be a change and give up the attempt at relocation. Relocation failure was a disappointment to face. After saving money for three years, I felt saddened and regretful to see planned expectations of an ideal new home cascading into oblivion. To me, the relocation was God–directed, and how could I have just made an enormous folly of it all? There were many questions about what I had been doing and thinking for those three years of planning. This type of letdown in the simple idea of moving to a new home shakes one to their foundation and makes for severe inward questioning. My concern was that should my time come to pass on, I would go to heaven. I was thinking about how my Christian friend had informed me that to go to heaven, a person must be saved. During this previous conversation, I asked her how to accomplish being saved. She answered merely to pray and ask Jesus.

Covering all bases and making sure I was going to heaven, I prayed to Jesus. Praying to our Jesus, asking Him for salvation was not in desperation but matter–of–factly. I knew whatever was needed to be heaven–bound would be where divine and fruitful efforts occur, unlike the current state, which was a colossal fiasco in wasted time and resources. I asked Jesus if it was indeed my time to go. Should this be the case, it was perfectly okay, and there was no worry, but it would be nice to know. I could attend last minute tasks in making a will and speaking with people for the last time. Supplications were about asking for heaven to please be the destination. My prayers to Jesus were also about being saved, should I need this to go to heaven, as my Christian friend had told me? Whatever being saved was, I asked for this to have heaven as my eternal home when the time came. I had confidence that whatever needed to be done for me to be saved would occur, and my eternal living place would be in heaven.

I still kept contentment with calmness in figuring out the following things to be accomplished in making the drive back from where I had come. Not everything in life goes as planned.

I believed that salvation and a way to heaven would prepare sometime, should this be required. And I knew these events would take place in moving forward for the proper education and enlightenment. I knew this might be through Christianity or another spiritual journey. It was January 30, 2010. I have discovered since, this was a sanctified and holy Sabbath, a seventh day of the week.

Sublime Choice

The next moment, while praying to Jesus, I felt intense energy throughout my body. It interrupted the petitions. I couldn't figure out what it meant when it was such a powerful vibration. It had a definite, intense effect; one that I was actively resisting. And to think now, I may have committed the unpardonable sin of grieving the Comforter Holy Spirit. This could have been a severe condition in losing salvation forever. Still, Jesus covered me and did what was necessary, not allowing any resistance to my placement into open vision,

Lord Jesus: Relax and let it flow.

I let the Holy Spirit's energy flow. There could be nothing but to obey as I saw Him as a glowing, white–robed figure, but not clearly in detailed facial features. Jesus was behind me and on my left side slightly. He sounded healthy, secure, at ease, and commanding in authority.

Yet, He was soft, affectionate, kind, and caring with His enrapturing tone and speech. In response to "Relax and let it flow," I took deep breaths with my mouth closed and my head tilted slightly back.

Sitting up straight, with respect, I purposefully relaxed my shoulders and my complete body while breathing deeply with slow exhales in trusting obedience. I heard Jesus' resonant, smooth, assuring voice, which caused me to obey promptly and willingly with deep-seated trust and love. The vibration produced euphoria in all areas of my being (physical, emotional, spiritual and mental) as the Holy Spirit took charge and expressed itself. I did not know what it was. Before this phenomenon, I had not known that the Holy Spirit existed.

Sweet little birdies gathered at the window. They were birds from the outside area, flitting and fluttering in joyful chaos. All the birds serenaded together happily, making beautiful music as they sang their sweet song to me. Within their happy chirping and chorus, there were words repeated over and over:

> ♪♪ *Come with us; we love you.*
> *Come with us; we love you.* ♪♪

Imagine forty birds fluttering sweetly and happily at the window. They were vertical, with tail feathers spread in a dangling, helicopter mode. Their wings flapped wildly to maintain their positions. As one would dart out, another would take its place. They kept coming and going. The activity was sweetly chaotic and joyous for me.

I listened closely and kept making sure of what I heard. Yes, it was perfectly understandable hearing the feathered creatures sing within their tweeting melodies, "Come with us; we love you." I wondered how it could be happening. It appeared to be a miracle because the words were so plain. I decided it was a miracle and a pleasant one to hear and watch. The miracle was what Jesus provided, so I thanked Him for it.

I told the birdies I loved them too, but how could I go with them when they have wings to fly, and I do not have wings and cannot fly? I thanked them and told them I loved them so much for the invitation and for thinking of me with kindness and enthusiasm—wherever they were going.

Opposite from the window and birds was the door. The screen door was closed with the outer door open to let in the morning sunlight and any warmth it might bring. Outside, a loud noise drew my attention as I heard two loudly rumbling and roaring war jets approaching low to the ground and right nearby. These types of jets were not an unusual sight in western desert areas. I had observed them before in their masterful takeoff and landing practices.

I saw two F–22 Raptors. They were dark, low, and exact in their close flyby. They pounded the ground, rumbling and shaking everything as they passed by with their thunderous roar. The trailer shook to where it would seem to come apart. Jesus made a profoundly eternal statement of command to me,

Lord Jesus: Make your choice.

O, how I love listening to the sound of His captivating voice! I thought carefully about what choice Jesus had specified. I didn't know at first. Then, through discernment given by our Lord Jesus, I understood it was the choice between darling birdies singing their acceptance, love and invitation—and war machines with all they represented in our world. I laughed, happy to make such a significant commitment because there was no choice. Smiling at Him a moment, with my chin lowered to my chest, I shook my head back and forth, laughing in humorous facetiousness. I told my Lord,

Snowye: What choice? There is no choice!

Formation Flight

Photo By: Air Force Staff Sgt.
James Richardson

Air Force F-22 Raptors fly in formation during training over the Joint Pacific Alaska Range Complex in Alaska, July 18, 2019.
The appearance of U.S. Department of Defense (DoD) visual information does not imply or constitute DoD endorsement.

I accepted the birds' melodious song of sweet invitation. I gave thanks and loved them in return for what they represented in sweet innocence and goodness. Humankind's ways on earth shown symbolically by the F–22's demonstrative flying were no comparison to spending eternity in heaven. Despite their majesty and power, the warplanes represented many of the undeniably alarming end–time events and grievances entangled with humanity. Wondering about what was going on, I asked Jesus how He was there? How could I see Him and still see and be aware of my physical surroundings? I pondered and asked Him how words could be within the birds' songs? His response was kind and tender in giving me clarification for this information I heartily wanted to understand,

Lord Jesus: Do not worry. Everything
               is fine and as it should be.
               Also, you have no breath.

The statement about my breath was a part that used to be left out when I shared what transpired because I thought no one would believe me, since it made no sense to me. It was momentous for me when I learned that people have their eyes open and have no breath when in an open vision. Along with being unusually weak, then ensuing with unusual strength, this state astonished medical doctors when they examined others as they were doing various acts while in a state of open vision experience.

> [3]Call unto me, and I will answer thee, and show thee great and mighty things, which thou knowest not.
> (Jeremiah 33:3)

Everyone is to have sufficient light to make
his decision intelligently.
  White, Ellen G.
  The Great Controversy, p. 605 (1911)

[5]Commit thy way unto the LORD; trust also
in him; and he shall bring it to pass.
  (Psalms 37:5)

His Hallowed Cross

Security, calmness, closeness and love were present during the complete instance. I had neither concept nor discernment of what He meant about my not having any breath. My attention went to my chest, wondering what this involved. Looking to observe whether there was any movement from breathing was a momentary distraction. By this time, the Holy Spirit took me at Jesus' command (it was an instant transition) to learn about His sacrifice for all humankind on His holy cross. I quickly forgot any contemplation on my breathing.

Romans constructed Jesus' cross with a crossbeam (Latin: *patibulum*) and what is called the stipes—the vertical beam of a cross used for crucifixion. *Stipes* can also mean a tree trunk, but this wasn't what I saw.

It was like being right there. My viewpoint was from Jesus' right side of the cross, resting my stomach across the patibulum, facing the stipes, with my right arm stretched along my right side, toward my feet. My left arm was extended forward, with my chin on the crossbeam. The perspective looked across the cross's left side (His left) out into the countryside with hills in the distance.

Turning my head to the right, I attempted to see what I heard below. People were amid slow and solemn activity with sadness, crying, and whimpering. Prayers recited by them while rocking on their knees were constant. They were kneeling and holding together in sorrow and emotional pain with their covered heads bowed in the litany and dressed in dark cloaks. I could hear the soldiers gambling and making rough talk with intermittent vulgar shouts and swearing.

I could see small but intense angst, born involuntarily out of appallingly agonizing torment. Jesus Christ tried not to move while on the cross. Still, Jesus couldn't help it because just breathing brought strain and a resulting involuntary movement, which brought on countless–sourced, misery–causing spasms in a never–ending cycle that resulted in utterly abject torture. These excruciating torments in response to His agony were from many places all over His body. He maintained dignity the entire exhaustive time in His utter love and strength. It made me weep then, and it still does to think about what He went through for us and the world.

I deeply wanted to extend relief to Him while at the same time, I knew none could be found. The impact touched me acutely with helplessness, and I profoundly felt compassion that was consuming and overwhelming. My thought was to extend comfort by dropping my right hand and touching His right–hand fingers, which I could have done. But I did not perform this action because this would have caused more of the miserable, intense agony He was already enduring in abysmal suffering. Compromising and wishing assuagement, I imparted considerable love in worship with my hand as close to His hand as possible without touching Him. I wanted to look and see

Him entirely, beyond the tips of the long and bloody thorns on His mournful head.

Lord Jesus: You are not able to look.
              I do not want you to see.
              It is too horrible to look at.

He revealed I could not look and perceive His self thoroughly on the cross. Unquestionably, this was so and not allowed. Though I desired to see, I could not, and it would not occur. My view turned along the patibulum in front of me and out into the countryside distance. This vision was of the profile of Christ Jesus, facing to the right. His bodily form and condition were as though He were on the cross. Jesus was on the cross, floating above the ground, up in the air. His arms were up and out, His chin on His chest, His knees bent. Viewing Him was far enough into the distance, I couldn't see the specifics of His horrific state. Truly He did not want His appalling condition seen by me.

Jesus showed the personal connection to His Father at all times in gloriousness. The link was a broad ray of bright, white splendor that shone on Jesus only and entirely. The beam of light stretched vertically from our Father to Himself. Jesus then showed me the removal of the light beam, His connection to His Father. Father's illumination didn't touch Jesus anymore. The gleam of brilliance remained above Him quite far up, leaving a wide gap. The beam of radiant light was Jesus' unique linkage to His eternal Father, full of love, mercy, grace, and all everlasting righteousness; revealed to me through discernment.

The entire world's evil poured onto and into Christ Jesus when He let go of our Father's brilliance. It was excruciatingly painful on all levels for Him, beyond comprehension. There is no portrayal of what it is like for a holy innocent to let go of heavenly paradise and our Father, and instantly have Satan's disgusting, evil wrath, with the world's sins descending and agonizingly manifest on all levels of Jesus' pure being.

I sensed this was the worst part of the ordeal of His sacrifice for us. It was worse than His agonizing spasms of torture on the sacred cross, as revealed to me through discernment from our Jesus.

Lord Jesus: Do not worry. It is all okay now.
              And this is all in the past.

He wanted me to know that I wasn't there during the authentic event when it occurred in the past. There was a titanic, roaring jolt of an earthquake. I heard it go throughout the world. Bedrock split apart with an intense, ear–shattering crack, creating a massive, long chasm in the ground. The sound of bedrock breaking apart was powerful, fierce, and sharp. The earthquake's released energy had everyone knowing He was the Son of God. I heard a man shout, "Truly, He is the Son of God!"

In the distance, coming extremely fast and high, so they hid the sky with no sunlight, were billowing, gigantic, rolling clouds of black darkness. They were potent because the clouds were enveloping and consuming all in their path with powerful, grinding turmoil, sending dirt high into the air. I have since learned these were clouds of angels.

The women screamed in terror at the foot of the cross as they viewed the darkness coming in. The deep blackness was all–encompassing. There was vehement thunder and lightning crackle (no rain) as the fierce wind blew and howled. It was difficult to move.

Men were yelling, and they all were shouting, "run, run!" A woman pleaded for them not to leave without them. They could not see their way and could not stand up because of the wind. No one could.

The men repeatedly shouted, "The women, help get the women!" Those small groups of men and women trying to leave, slowly moved as they felt their way along the trail. They were on their hands and knees, crawling closely together as best they could. The blowing dirt, pebbles, and opaque darkness made it so no one went very far, although it was their intense desire.

They crept on their knees, determinedly, inch–by–inch, helping each other, trying to stand and falling instead. However, their progress was only a few feet, so they were still at the base of His hallowed cross. They covered themselves with their robes and lay there holding together to protect from hurt against the blowing dirt, sand, rubble, and grits. The wind settled. There was whimpering with soft crying in fear at the foundation of His cross. The foot of His cross is all I could pay attention to in my direct view. There were consoling words and assurances with comforting prayers. They spoke tender words with whispers revealing what beautiful, kind, and virtuous people they were.

Lord Jesus: I did this for you and the whole world.
I am connected again to My
Father with the light.

Lord Jesus: Do not worry; I am alright now,
and it will never happen again.

Snowye: Yes, My Lord.

[21]For he hath made him to be sin for us, who knew no sin; that we might be made the righteousness of God in him.
(II Corinthians 5:21)

His Elegant Grace and Mercy

Then Jesus took me to another place after His holy cross. It was an instant transition to a large rock face. We were kneeling together on the ground, praying as we leaned against the boulder with our shoulders touching it. As we were facing, holding hands, Lord Jesus was speaking soft, reverent appeals.

After the prayers ended, we sat down by the rock, still enjoying its warmth. Dear Jesus brushed all the dirt off a metal box as He turned it in His hands and showed it to me. He then set the box on the ground. He was tenderly and slowly taking a file card out of the eight by five–inch metal file box. My Jesus handed slowly, with reverence, cards for me to hold, one at a time. We intensely examined each card's details. He sweetly and quietly revealed every commandment that I had ever broken in my entire sin–filled lifetime with a card.

I viewed all incidents on the cards as if I were watching a full–color movie with sound, close–ups, and zooming long shots on a video screen embedded in the card. Jesus would gently point out each of my debts, transgressions, iniquity, and sin since my birth. He did this with astounding loving kindness, tenderness, and compassion. He would mention with each card,

Lord Jesus: Look and see. This is how the (e.g., second)
              commandment was broken. He then fully
              recited the commandment. Remember
              when (video watched), do you see?
Snowye: Yes, my Lord.

We watched each video with heightened scrutiny to the many
details surrounding all the broken commandments in my lifetime,
astoundingly from when I was born.

Lord Jesus: You now understand how you broke
              the (e.g., fourth) commandment?
Snowye: Yes, my Lord.
Lord Jesus: You promise not to do it again and break
              the (e.g., fourth) commandment, right?
Snowye: Yes, I promise not to do it. And I
              promise I will not break the (e.g.,
              fourth) commandment again.

Each card showed individual video incidents in full color and
sound, just like watching a DVD. I made the very solemn promise
not to break that commandment again. It was all about a lifetime
of incidences where I broke each of the Ten Commandments
countless times.

Amazingly, my life was recorded like this for viewing. It
must be the same for all of us—something I think about with
books in heaven and God's omniscience!

After Jesus and I initially reviewed five cards, the
entirety of the individual cards and the conversation about it
passed quickly, like my life flashing before my eyes. It took

a little while to accomplish the entire grave responsibility. I realized afterward that it was a somber and dignified rite. The impression of each card was strongly and distinctly made. I was to obey and be in harmony with God's eternal law. Since the vision, it has been my highest priority in all my actions and passions to obey and follow Father's eternal summary of His law, the Ten Commandments.

Jesus was in a maroon robe, with a beige undergarment/tunic and brown leather sandals. From sitting, we positioned ourselves to kneel on the ground and prayed together by the large boulder that juts out from surrounding smoother and darkened bedrock. The rock's reserved warmth from sunlight was comforting. It created a retreat with the boulder on one side and a tree shading the area's other side. Large bushes surrounded and completed the comfortable privacy. Praying with Jesus was memorable and gratifying because His presence was calming, peaceful, and assuring. I learned later that we were in the Garden of Gethsemane, where He sweat drops of blood in prayers to His Father before the crucifixion, gaining strength and courage as angels ministered to Him. To think that He shared this with me brings an eternal love for Him in my heart.

Jesus taught me the Lord's Prayer and Psalms 23. He alternated, giving me the choices of reciting either debt/debtors or transgressions/transgressors. Jesus lovingly and tenderly repeated the prayers many times for me to memorize. He was a stern teacher, not letting me forget, and He waited until I thoroughly learned them.

The doxology ("for thine is the kingdom, the power, and the glory, forever. Amen") was not in the Lord's Prayer that Jesus was teaching me. I found out later that Christians in the eastern half of the Roman Empire and Greek scribes copying scripture added the doxology afterward for various reasons. Jesus emphasized many times the way to end the Lord's Prayer was with "the Evil One" instead of "evil."

Doxology

In the early Church, the Christians living in the eastern half of the Roman Empire added the doxology "for thine..." to the Gospel text of the Our Father when reciting the prayer at Mass. Evidence of this practice is also found in the "Didache" (Teaching of the Twelve Apostles), a first century manual of morals, worship and doctrine of the Church. Also, when copying the Scriptures, Greek scribes sometimes appended the doxology onto the original Gospel text of the Our Father, however, most texts today would omit this inclusion, relegate it to a footnote, or note that it was a later addition to the Gospel. Official "Catholic" Bibles including the Vulgate, the Douay–Rheims, the Confraternity Edition, and the New American have never included this doxology.

From: STRAIGHT ANSWERS
By Fr. William Saunders
Who Added the Doxology?
https://www.ewtn.com/catholicism/
library/who-added-the-doxology-1002
(Accessed May 6, 2022)

Lord's Prayer (Version taught to me by Jesus)

> Our Father which art in heaven, Hallowed be thy name. Thy kingdom come. Thy will be done in earth, as in heaven. Give us this day our daily bread. And forgive us our debts, as we forgive our debtors. And lead us not into temptation, but deliver us from the Evil One. Amen.

After memorizing the prayers, another instant transition was provided, and I was bowed at His feet as He stood before me. Jesus had returned to wearing His white robe. Prostration was something that occurred without volition and as a command. However, to bow wasn't verbalized as a command. Bowing at His feet simply transpired. It was the most lovely, joyous honor and privilege to be prostrated low before our Lord and Savior. Many moments passed with my kneeling, forehead touching the soil, palms on the ground, and fingers extended just beyond my head with elbows bent in contented honor and worship of Lord Jesus. I wished these moments would have never ended. I knew Jesus deserved all worship, and He was worthy of the humble adoration and praise that everyone should be willingly giving Him. He is noble, stately, majestic, our powerful Creator and Redeemer, Lord Jesus, the Son of God.

I couldn't help the inclination and action because I wanted to see Him. Slowly and carefully, I raised my head and eyes just enough to see His feet. His beautiful feet, clad in leather sandals, held the scars of crucifixion, and there was a most glorious white aura emanating strongly from inside His being. The radiating glow from Him is warm, gratifying, accepting and dear to behold.

[6]O come, let us worship and bow down: let us kneel before the LORD our maker.
(Psalms 95:6)

[8]I will keep thy statutes: O forsake me not utterly.
(Psalms 119:8)

[10]With my whole heart I have sought thee: O let me not wander from thy commandments.
(Psalms 119:10)

[10]Create in me a clean heart, O God; and renew a right spirit within me.
(Psalms 51:10)

[13]Let us hear the conclusion of the whole matter: Fear God, and keep his commandments: for this is the whole duty of man.
(Ecclesiastes 12:13)

[10]For we must all appear before the judgment seat of Christ; that every one may receive the things done in his body, according to that he hath done, whether it be good or bad.
(II Corinthians 5:10)

[15]If ye love me, keep my commandments.
(John 14:15)

Holy Visage

I couldn't help it. I wanted to see more of Jesus than the bowing position allowed. Mulling it over in introspection, I searched for the courage to ask permission to see His face. He seemed to know what I wanted.

Lord Jesus: Would you like to see my face?

Snowye: Yes, please!

He leaned over and took both my hands, helping me first to upright kneeling and then to standing. I stood up slowly to memorize Lord Jesus entirely as much as possible, from feet to head. A large scar was on top of His left foot. His sandals are a simple, functional design with no big toe loop made from elegant, finely–tanned, robust and smooth leather.

The fabric of His robe was stunning. It was even, finely and tightly woven, soft, cashmere–like wool. The robe's white color was a slightly creamier white than the whiter light that emanates and glows from inside His complete beloved being. His robe flows and drapes into sophisticated folds, providing plenteous room for movement. Cut in a relaxed, simple, and stately manner, it looked comfortable. There was no undergarment visible at the hem. His robe reached to mid ankle. The long sleeves of His robe draped from His wrists, then widened in a cut designed to do this. Flowing fabric from His wrists was long and distinguished. The large mantle/shawl ("himation" in Greek), made of the same material as His robe, draped elegantly in neat, and lovely gathers. Jesus' mantle went from His right shoulder to drape over His left hip.

He held me this way, with my hands in His, as I gazed into His face, especially His glistening eyes, memorizing love, bliss, joy, and breathtaking elation. What a gorgeous smile He had! There was a slight breeze blowing onto His face so that his hair lifted and went out from His head a little. His hair is not stringy like so many depictions. Instead, it is lush, thick, and shiny with beautiful waves from the top of His head to the end of His tresses. Jesus' hair, parted in the middle, extended to just below His shoulders, was trimmed neatly and splendidly. His hair is radiant in shining, vibrant healthfulness.

His impeccable and healthful complexion glowed in wholesome color. Lord Jesus' full beard was neatly trimmed to perfection, shiny and thick. His full–of–depth, green eyes emanating significance and love were eternally captivating. I thought His eyes would be brown and wondered if He did this for me because my eyes are green. But no was the answer. When looking into His eyes, they sparkled, pouring out indescribable love with different brown, gold, orange, yellow, and blue colors. The love that emanates from His glittering eyes is full of acceptance and devotion. The compassion, caring, and kindness reached deeply into my whole being and soul. It was glorious to realize that I was standing there, holding hands with my Lord and Savior, Jesus Christ. I experienced His tremendous love that I cannot wholly describe—only that it is all anyone could ever want—forever.

Jesus is stately, and looking at Him was exceptional! Gazing at Jesus' face was deeply fulfilling on all levels. Long moments passed with being enveloped in intimate love, compassion, approval, and kindness. He let go of my hands and stepped back a few steps from me. He held his hands open, palms slightly up, showing them to me with His arms stretched outwardly from His sides in a pose of divine humility. He sweetly asked in humility, coinciding with a great sureness of confidence, expertise, and authority,

Lord Jesus: Is there anything more I can do for you?

The question caught me by surprise. I was unprepared to answer. The impression was, to my wonder, that anything I asked would be fully granted. I thought of earthly wealth but rejected the idea because it was unsuitable to request this when Jesus' presence is all anyone could ever desire. Glowing health, well–being for me and all I knew was one of my ideas. Quite a few moments passed in pondering many scenarios, knowing I could take all the time I wanted to think it over. There was no hurry with Jesus' patience in His waiting for an answer. It was challenging to decide what I would request, so my meditation wandered to what other people in my life might lack. I discerned, for the time being, that earthly peace for humankind was not yet to be played out in Father's perfect plan.

Then the thought occurred to me, and it clicked in my mind that it might be accomplished now, when never at any other time. I was so excited that I couldn't wait to ask! It was something that I had always wanted!

Snowye: Can I see God's face too?

Jesus' reaction confused me. He wholeheartedly and outwardly leaned back and laughed as He was genuinely joyous with this request. Thinking He could place a picture inside my mind's eye to know what God looked like was the idea, or possibly God's face could be shown in a painting or photograph. Maybe Jesus could have the clouds turn into a likeness of our Father. These were my hopes and ideas to see our Creator's face. I was surprised by Jesus' vigorous laughter in what I was hoping was pleasure and that everything was still okay while waiting for a response of yes or no. I became fatigued, and I asked Him if I could go lie down on the bed.

Lord Jesus: Yes. Go to the bed and lie down.

The idea was to close my eyes and rest for a while. Jesus said with sternness and chastised me like a loving father when I attempted to shut my eyes,

Lord Jesus: Your eyes will remain open.
Snowye: Yes, my Lord.

We shot up through the clouds fast. It was a far distance that took a bit of time. I no longer had any awareness of our physical earth and resting on the bed. We stopped to look at the limitless number of stars in adoration of their beauty. There was love and joy always felt with our Jesus. Lord Jesus is love.

Lord Jesus: Behold the stars; each has a name.
Snowye: All of them have names?
              There are so many!

It was incomprehensible that so many stars existed, and each one had its unique name. Discernment produced that this included an identity and a personality for each one. As contemplation took place on this mystery, we continued away from the beautiful stars to grasp that there could be this many stars, let alone so many names. God is marvelous. The Almighty is good. God cares. It was a wonder to think that not one star of the gazillions (more than this?) was missing its name. Like the 7.9 billion humans on earth, in addition to the multitudes in their graves, I am sure God knows all our names and every tiny detail about us. He cares about us in specifics and minutiae that cannot be comprehended by a human being's mind. We are created and treated like precious individuals who matter to the utmost.

> [4]He telleth the number of the stars; he calleth them all by their names.
>   (Psalms 147:4)

> [6]By the word of the LORD were the heavens made; and all the host of them by the breath of his mouth.
>   (Psalms 33:6)

5

Footpath Like None Other

Where this charming trail led that Lord Jesus, and I strolled on–I didn't know. It was an enjoyable walk with a simple trust in Him. Whatever we were doing was terrific, acceptable and satisfactory to me. We walked hand–in–hand, side–by–side on a lane edged with grass and splendidly flowering bushes. I saw fully leafed, lush, and tall trees in all directions. The dry dirt path (no dust) was in a wild terrain that expanded on both sides with low grass, leading to the pine tree forest defining its random edge. The sun shone brightly, warming the sweet air as butterflies and birds flickered around us on all sides. They would dance up to us, then leave and come flying back. The sunshine came through the trees in shining beams and rays. Birdsong was in the air, with fresh scents of trees, bark, leaves, and perfumed blossoms. It was a paradise. We walked happily, enjoying the surroundings for many miles this way. Lord Jesus was one with all the wildlife and plants as they reacted with joy when He walked past them. There was a thorough delight all along the way, and all life gave homage to Him with their petite behaviors. Plants leaned toward Him, and animals came up with love to gain His attention if they could fly near Him closely or joyfully cross His (and my) path.

We walked up to a striking geographical feature that resembled a large bowl. It comprised evenly–cut green plush grass. Neatly trimmed, the grass was two feet tall, and was a rich green color. The grass bowl was a natural depression and part of the terrain. The footpath followed the top rim of the grass bowl to the left. The pathway was beside a mountain and continued, making a horseshoe shape on the bowl's top edge, over to the opposite side, where the trail was beside another mountain. You could go straight ahead, down the bowl's curved side, and up the other side to pick up the track as a shortcut when first approaching the grass bowl. The other two sides (the left and right sides approaching the grass bowl) were open to remarkable fathomless abysses.

Alan was standing just off the grass bowl path at the end of the horseshoe shape. He was in the bowl a bit from where the track picked up on the other side. My Lord and God, Jesus, continued walking to the left, along the top edge. It was an upward walk to the left toward this highest part of the grass bowl's perimeter. The portion of the footpath we were coming to bordered an abyss of an indescribable, colossal expanse. Jesus walked ahead and stood at this highest part of the bowl's trail/path/rim. He walked silently. The leather of Jesus' sandals was broken in properly for no squeak of the leather or for making a flapping sound. His manly stride was adept, graceful, purposeful, powerful, noble, and full of astonishing grandeur.

The Power of God

He did not move when He reached the top edge of the grass bowl's rim, waiting for me. Jesus looked out over the expanse in a stoical pose. Jesus stood dignified, composed, self–assured, and relaxed in noble and grave contemplation. His robe and hair would flow behind Him in the wind. The wind would break and then come back. Each time, His garments blew backward, His robe and hem trailing far behind and upward from His ankles. Jesus' hair blew away from His face to behind His shoulders. He was a powerful, imposing sight.

Jesus turned and helped me up the last of the way, stretching His arm out and gripping my hands because I took a shortcut through the grass to reach Him faster. There we stood together, but not holding hands. We moved to ten feet apart, at the top crescent of this horseshoe–shaped trail. We were looking out over a colossal expanse of cloud cover. Lord Jesus was glorious, complete in purpose and ability that could be plainly and marvelously observed in how He majestically stood there.

Deep purple mountain tops peeked through the cloud cover in the infinite distance. The immeasurable space of the monumental view inspired awe. The clouds we were looking over expanded across the vast, far–reaching region. Their color was the deep gray of rain clouds and cumulonimbus (thunder cloud). It was comforting and empowering to stand there. We looked out over the clouds and listened to the wind giving its unique sound as it passed over the tops of pine trees below us in smooth and flowing waves. I had always cherished this rich whooshing and rushing sound of wind through the treetops.

I heard a rumbling, low, and serene roll with lightning crackles and the wind's sounds. A grid rose from within the cloud cover. The grid of squares comprised light–blue lightning and had periodic crackles and the movement of lightning along the lines making up its fascinating structure. As it rose, the grid lit up the clouds. The grid slowly rose to where it could be observed and then it slowly descended, rising and falling in slow, rhythmic regularity. The grid's size was enormous. The squares had four–hundred–mile sides. As the grid rose, the wind blew on my Lord. As the grid subsided, so did the current, of which Jesus was visibly a part. The sounds of lightning crackle and thunder increased and were loud as the grid rose into view. This sound decreased as it fell back into the clouds where we didn't see it and we barely heard it. It is beyond wonderment, as it slowly and smoothly would rise to view and then gradually reduce back into the clouds where it disappeared.

Jesus turned and seriously looked me straight in the eyes. He stretched out His left arm toward the clouds and grid in a powerful pose. His left hand was wide open, fingers spread, bent upward at the wrist. He was a riveting sight with the intensity in His eyes. His long robes were wildly flowing in the wind. He said to me in all stalwartness, powerfulness, reverence, and solemnity,

Lord Jesus: Behold.
              The Power of God.

I beheld. Looking out, falling to my knees as Jesus did in respect, devotion, and marvelous love, we both were praying. We worshiped our unparalleled Father as we reverently overlooked The Power of God.

We stood up. Jesus took my left hand into His right hand. Jesus guided me into the grass bowl below. We were standing still, holding hands, my left arm and His right arm outstretched. Alan had been slowly walking up to us all this time. Alan was there to take my other (right) hand into his left to hold. Jesus,' Alan's, and my arms were fully extended. We were inside the grass bowl with Jesus near the top rim, where we had been viewing the Power of God, worshiping and praying on our knees together in respect and complete awe.

> [18] The voice of thy thunder was in the heaven: the lightnings lightened the world: the earth trembled and shook. [19] Thy way is in the sea, and thy path in the great waters, and thy footsteps are not known.
> (Psalms 77:18, 19)

Healing Through Our Lord

My Lord and God, Christ Jesus, reached out to stretch His left arm and upward hand toward the cloud cover and electrical grid—the Power of God. His garments flew, swirling in the heavy wind. His hem, sleeves, and hair were in a wild tempest and exhibited mighty fortitude as He looked toward the Power of God. He stood firmly and steadily. He bent His left knee toward the higher side of the curved grass bowl and stood determinedly against the robust whipping wind. While all three of us were still holding hands, Jesus turned his head toward me with our arms outstretched. He leaned forward to seriously and intently look into my eyes with His serious, penetratingly profound, and powerful gaze,

Lord Jesus: This is how you heal.

Jesus and Alan let go of my hands after a few moments. My Lord returned up to the edge through the grass. He stood for a moment, viewing the Power of God. Jesus started walking the grass bowl's rim, following the horseshoe shape to the other side, where the trail was alongside another mountain. I watched our majestic Lord Jesus as He was rounding this awe–inspiring footpath.

Waters of Delicate Song

He stopped and dipped into the spring's rock–hewn bowl inside a small cave. The cave was carved roughly into darkly colored basalt rock. Jesus took a drink and continued making His way by walking the dirt footpath. I ran to look at the spring and be with Him, intent not to get lost and left behind.

He turned and came back. Jesus showed me the spring inside the small cave. He spoke of how it was forever crystal clear, renewed itself, and remained flowing there. He presented the stone–carved cup as He held it. The cup was a simple design with no stem or handle and comfortably rested in His curved palm. He then placed it back in a spot made for it to rest. It was a flat rock ledge carved for it inside the small cave. The cup's rock ledge jutted out a little over the tranquil pool of cool, pure, refreshing water.

The little cave makes a rare song. He said it is called Owin Spring. The vibration of the small waterfall inside the cave that feeds the pool creates a tiny echo. The echo reverberation has its own graceful and lovely harmonizing tune and song. The shape and location of the small cave acts as amplification. Its wonderful music cascaded throughout the area.

I discerned this was a stopping point for cleansing and drinking for sustenance to continue on the path. Jesus had lifted me to a rounded boulder to stand on in order to see inside. Thinking to take a drink, He said sweetly,

Lord Jesus: The water is not for you to drink at this time.

I did not know why the water from Owin Spring was not for me to drink. Possibly it was because those who drank from Owin Spring would "… go back to earth no more…" like a similar explanation Prophet Ellen G. White describes below in what Jesus said about "… Those who eat of the fruit of this land go back to earth no more…"

> I asked Jesus to let me eat of the fruit. He said, "Not now. Those who eat of the fruit of this land go back to earth no more. But in a little while, if faithful, you shall both eat of the fruit of the tree of life and drink of the water of the fountain." And He said, "You must go back to the earth again and relate to others what I have revealed to you."…
> White, Ellen G.
> *Early Writings*, pp. 19, 20

[14]But whosoever drinketh of the water that I shall give him shall never thirst; but the water that I shall give him shall be in him a well of water springing up into everlasting life. (John 4:14)

Jesus retook my left hand into His affectionate clasp. We walked to where the footpath completed its horseshoe shape and continued to the left. The grass bowl and the paradise trail remained behind us.

I asked if Alan would go with us because I would have liked that. Alan was already making way through the bowl of green grass and walking back toward what was like a trail of paradise.

Lord Jesus: Alan will be staying.
              He does not want to go right now.

His Luminous Footsteps

We continued to hold hands at the end of the horseshoe shape and made the left turn. Some space and ground carpeted with short grass were on both sides. It dropped off into another bottomless crevasse on the right. A high rising mountain of rock was on the left. The dirt passage gradually narrowed. Incrementally and progressively, the ground checked on both sides, giving way to a much smaller trail cut into the rock mountainside that was only approximately sixteen inches wide.

Still holding Jesus' hand, I dropped behind Him but kept mindfully attentive as we walked. The path was cut into the stone mountainside. The drop–off on the right was straight down for what must have been many miles. I could see nothing in that void except deep purple darkness and a few swirling, misty wisps of thin white clouds. This drop–off on the right was sheer and immediate. The rock mountainside on the left was form–shaped, so it was slightly wider at shoulder height.

The footpath became only six inches wide for any walking space. There was just enough room to place one foot in front of the other. I was barefoot, trusting Jesus' firm and attentive hold on my hand as we made our way along this extremely precarious and narrow pathway.

Sunlight disappeared slowly, and dimness was setting in like a fading sunset. Continuing on the footpath, it became darker in a gradual process that had coincided with the path becoming narrower. Still only six inches wide, this passage was a dangerous trek. After a while, there was no light. Absolute pitch–black came on us so that I could not see one thing in any direction. Even His white robe was not visible. He continued holding my hand as we placed one foot in front of the other, walking the straight and narrow, now in complete, opaque, pitch–blackness.

The marvel that made walking in this situation possible was the glowing, holy light emanating from His sandaled feet. The radiant glow went no farther than His hem, illuminating the path under and near His feet. This glowing, warm light was just enough for Him to know where to place His next careful step, and the same with mine.

The feeling of security and safety never left me. When I asked how long the path was, Jesus told me it would be a very long distance on the narrow, mysterious trail. I was content, and time was unimportant because I was so happy and filled with trust and security. Only the task of carefully placing each footstep mattered. How many miles long was this unlit and tight part of the route? Guessing would be impossible, and there was no way of telling. I did not know where we were going, and it did not matter. He gave me a discerning perspective of one–hundred and twenty miles when I inwardly wondered how far we were going.

Jesus paused from walking a moment. The full impact of realization took root in my being. I acutely comprehended the abyss's proximity to the right and the sheer mountain rock on the left while in complete darkness. He clasped my hand in both of His as He turned toward me. His white aura shone so I could see Him as He looked into my face. Held by Him in this secure way, He said,

Lord Jesus: I will never let you go.

This profound moment was a tender interaction with assurance that I would be His child throughout eternity. I realized that, indeed—He could let go. The thought that He could let go was admittedly an alarming one. Not so much the realization that we were on a tiny, dark path, with a sheer abyss on one side and no light brought forth, aside from He—but the relationship, companionship, love; therefore, any meaning for My Life might end. Losing all sense of meaningful life alarmed me with the thought of His letting go. I expressed a passionate plea to my Lord,

Snowye: No! Please never let go!

This moment was a formal agreement and pact. Intimate love held for My Lord and My Savior Jesus, to this moment, is consummate. I knew He would never forsake me, never leave me, never give up on me, and never reject me. I knew my Lord Jesus would always be there for me. Fulfillment and security with Him would eternally exist because I knew He genuinely loves me forever.

We continued our way on this tiny trail. It was a while later, and Jesus stopped again and turned toward me. This time, He took both of my hands into both of His. His grip was firm, warm, and secure. Our grasp was slightly tighter than before. Light emanated from His being so I could see His face. Looking into my eyes, He emphasized with one slight affirming shake of our clasped hands,

Lord Jesus: You are mine.

And, He is mine. It was a cherished, loving statement of fact. Unusual to describe, it was a command as well. I felt every bit of this belonging that I tremendously desired. I knew I was a part of Him, and He was a part of me. As though a beautiful solid rock was inside of me, I felt centered. It was as it should be in the overall of things for me, forever.

This oath was an exceptional covenant between the two of us. I am His, and He is mine. My allegiance in all ways is Lord Jesus' only; it always will be. Jesus Christ is my Chosen One. I consider it an honor to worship our Lord and Savior, Jesus.

An intense ambition to obey and please Jesus out of love is a deeply felt part of my entire existence that has not gone in all these years. He is near to me and there for me at all times.

Eternally and gratefully, there is peace, well–being, and security in His rewarding love.

[12]Then spake Jesus again unto them, saying, I am the light of the world: he that followeth me shall not walk in darkness, but shall have the light of life.
(John 8:12)

[5]And the light shineth in darkness; and the darkness comprehended it not.
(John 1:5)

[11]Cast me not away from thy presence; and take not thy holy spirit from me.
(Psalms 51:11)

[20]At that day ye shall know that I am in my Father, and ye in me, and I in you.
(John 14:20)

[1]But now thus saith the LORD that created thee, O Jacob, and he that formed thee O Israel, Fear not: for I have redeemed thee, I have called thee by thy name; thou art mine.
(Isaiah 43:1)

6

Behold. Gates of a Single Pearl

The narrow path gradually widened. It increasingly became warm and sunny, leaving all the darkness behind. It then opened to a broad, impressive, wondrous, and glorious sight of the loveliest terrain I had ever seen or knew could exist.

The footpath's edge overlooked an extensive domain, as if viewing a settlement coming out of the comfy woods. The tree line gave way to descending sloping hillsides of grass, spreading on both sides. Wildflowers and plants gave off pleasant rich scents in the lush green grass, which expanded far before us. There were different, more intense countryside colors: trees, rocks, bushes and flowers. Deer and other animals grazed and raised their heads to watch Jesus walking by. Bushes and rocks gleamed. It was like here on earth, but with extra jubilation, newness, largeness and brightness. Everything was alive and glowing with an aura of white light emanating from the rocks, plants, flowers, and animals. The wild countryside contained no debris, dried sticks, and leaves, nor lack of neatness, anywhere. All was tidy with charming randomness. The landscape was healthful and radiating visually with an elegant light of grandeur like what glowed from Jesus Christ's inner being.

Translucent Gold

We were approaching a smooth expanse with nothing on it. It separated the wild terrain we were in from the other side, where it was glowing and glittering all in white.

We began walking on the smooth expanse as we continued toward a gorgeous white city. The space we strolled on spanned many miles to the right and left, and many miles across until reaching the other side.

On the other side of the smooth expanse, the stunning white city walls were so high that the inside details of the city itself weren't visible. The walls glowed with white light and sparkled delicately and elegantly.

We stopped in the middle of the smooth area as Jesus still held my hand in His. He drew my awareness to where we were standing. Smiling, He said,

Lord Jesus: What we walk on is purest fine gold.
              Behold. You can see through it.

Looking below through the translucent gold was fabulous. We were over a massive, miles–deep canyon with a river winding and flowing at the bottom. The river was tiny from that height. A similar likeness would be like standing over the Grand Canyon and looking below, only much higher. The stunning construction of the see–through gold with the gorgeous whitish golden tint was commendable and admired. It was a bridge like none other.

I asked Jesus how the sheer gold held us because it would seem to bend or sink under our feet with gold's softness. Jesus showed me with discernment blueprint images with mathematical statements, algebraic/geometric formulas, and molecular diagrams that it contained a slight arch with the highest point in the middle. The arc was so gradual that walking on it was like a flat surface because it was so wide. He also explained that the molecular structure was vital for the purpose and that He and His Father made it that way.

The translucent golden bridge over a canyon is a Wonder of God. It is a beautiful, awe–inspiring masterpiece from God in His many incomparable and spectacular creations. Years later, from the biblical study, I ask myself if this fantastic golden bridge is the Sea of Glass.

Walls of the City

Still in the middle, on top of the sheer, see–through golden divide, Jesus turned to face the white–walled city. He positioned us to view the city from this perfect vantage point, His hands on my shoulders from behind. Showing to me toward the left, over toward the phenomenal, glittering walls, He said,

Lord Jesus: Behold the walls. They have all
colors of finest gems.

The walls were utterly spectacular. Subtly sparkling, the walls appeared white from top to bottom. Horizontal layers of subtle colors from the base's sparkling gems were absolutely beautiful.

The gem layers were exquisite, appearing primarily white because the gems were multifaceted. The facets reflected white light with only the palest touch of the gem's color. Heavy–duty, the glittering walls were massively thick, rising in splendor and impressiveness with their extreme height and solid build. They were unbelievably fabulous and dazzling to behold.

We crossed over to the other side of the translucent, finest gold bridge that spans a canyon. The edge of the sheer gold on the side we approached was where everything turned completely white. All was glowing with the same divine light that emanated from Jesus. The grass and ground were white, with a touch of sparkle. Trees and bushes, bark, and leaves were all glistening white. It enveloped this other side of the golden bridge in an exquisitely luminous white light, iridescent and beautiful. It was too lovely for expression. There were angels outside the walls, all in white attire, busy with various tasks, walking or talking with interest and thoughtful purpose. It was lovely to be there, with welcoming and warmth exuding from every direction.

I could hear music in melodious and harmonizing spiritual tones as we walked. The music radiated from very high above, and it spanned like a colossal arc all across the sky. One could hear the music if they paid attention to it; otherwise, it was a soothing background harmony. Listening closely, I noticed the chorus was made of individuals singing different unique melodies that combined into one glorious harmonizing opus that enraptured one to hear. Listening to any elegant individual piece could occupy a person's enthralled being forever.

Divine Portals of Pearl

Jesus stopped. Facing the gate in the gorgeous wall, He positioned me with His hands on my shoulders from behind. Jesus lovingly said,

Lord Jesus: Behold. The gate is one single pearl.

Only our God and Jesus could make a pearl as incredibly massive as this one. The gate, constructed of a single pearl with its white pearl essence, glows subtly, warmly and grandly. I inspected it, admiring its radiant white beauty. The pearl was richly smooth and slightly naturally–textured, and glowing with a touch of opalescence in colors. The luminous white pearl is breathtakingly gorgeous and tastefully complements the white walls with sparkling gems. The pearl gate was impressively tall, fitting perfectly into the towering city wall, making a solid, fortified entrance.

I cannot guess the actual height. We were teensy compared to the wall and the pearl gates within those walls. Jesus pointed out the sweet angel that stood as gatekeeper. The gatekeeper's height allowed him to operate the pearl gate. Jesus went up ahead and spoke with the angel. He then waited for me to come up to the entrance. I went up an earthen mound which turned into stone steps. With discernment, Jesus emphasized the gate was one pearl. It provides a mighty, impenetrable bastion with the arc strength of the convex shape and a pearl's durable mother–of–pearl material and construction.

Before the gate opened, Jesus showed a delicate and subtle grid pattern in a light, lime–green color of light. The grid was etched into the enormous pearl. I didn't notice it until it was lit up. This electrical grid is threadlike and contains much knowledge and data. I do not remember the function of the grid. Jesus explained the data to me with a direct download vision, but I didn't comprehend the details—only that it was vital. The grid was not visible until Jesus wanted it to be there. It stopped being lit up when He was through showing it.

The tall angel gatekeeper opened the richly lustrous pearl gate for Our Lord. This angel gave high reverence to Lord Jesus by slowly opening the gate. The angel opened sufficiently the pearl gate for Jesus to step through with me behind Him. I was wholly taking in every detail. Just inside the gate, Jesus stopped and spoke to me, giving assurance,

Lord Jesus: When we get inside, I will leave you for
              a few minutes. It will not be long.

Discernment revealed we would not be holding hands for a short while (precisely 5.6 minutes) and that I was to wait and not be afraid. The angel secured the enormous pearl gate effortlessly behind us, without a sound. Once inside, there was an area to wait. On the opposite wall from the pearl gate, the foyer had an arched tunnel entrance. The short tunnel connected the foyer to another colossal room. Our grand Creator assembled the short tunnel all from smooth, gray, stone blocks, including the floor.

There was no decor or furniture in the foyer, and the light source wasn't one I could detect. Jesus placed me on the far wall from the pearl gate, nearby the arched tunnel entry leading to the large room.

I stood on the stone and looked at the plain stone blocks of the tunnel's high walls and ceiling. I moved only my head and eyes, not daring to explore, nor take a step. Jesus left me and I stood right where he left me. The foyer's walls and ceiling were as high as the gate and the outside walls. I saw an ornate opening carved in the stone high near the top. Soon (5.6 minutes), Jesus came back to get me. We entered farther inside from the superb gate made of a single, priceless, gorgeous pearl.

> [21]And the twelve gates were twelve pearls: every several gate was of one pearl: and the street of the city was pure gold, as it were transparent glass.
> (Revelation 21:21)

Praise of Angels

Jesus and I walked inside, holding hands, weaving about and through the angels as they sang praises. Splendidly beyond words, the angels were worshiping, praying, singing, and chanting in orderly, glorious, striking unison that was never wanted to stop and captivated one to hear,

Angels: [8]... Holy, holy, holy, Lord God Almighty, which was, and is, and is to come.
(Revelation 4:8)

It was loud. It was joyous. The angels were alongside and pressed in on all sides of us. The essence of this holy gift from my Jesus is eternal and I will never forget as I strive to be worthy. Experiencing the angels was like being given a precious gift of Life.

The angels appeared like soldiers dressed in form fitting leather for top armor. Their Greek–style leather armor was in tasteful colors of reddish–brown and lighter browns. I noticed the angels' armor trimmed in pure gold. They wore sandals made from sable brown–colored leather, and the sandal straps crisscrossed up their calves to below their knees. Reddish–brown capes attached at each shoulder draped to their calves.

Some held a long rod or staff, and some had trumpets. The trumpets were more toward the front, but we still heard them as they sounded in great unison for emphasis at specific points in the revered display of devotion to our Father. They wore handsome gold helmets for headgear that were trimmed with gold filigree. I was so much smaller than these gigantic angels arrayed as an army. Listening to their worshipful praises was so uplifting that I never wanted hearing them to end.

These magnificent angels repeated many times the worshipful chanting and singing "Holy, Holy, Holy." They sang other supplications and variations of the declarations proclaimed as well. The allegiance, chants and pronouncements varied in their presentations. The praise of angels contained the following unified magnificence: Singing, strong promulgations, affirmations and statements, military–type sidestepping movement, an in–place stamp of the foot, in–place stamp of staffs on the floor, blowing of trumpets, a short and loud shout for great emphasis.

It was a resounding, divine, orderly, adoring praise to Almighty God. The angels' tribute is entirely enveloping to listen to, captivating, uplifting, and pure. No length of time could be adequate to realize, feel, and experience this utter splendidness as the angels acclaim our Lord God Almighty. My gratitude and thankfulness flow to all the angels and Lord Jesus, giving me this breathtaking enlightenment of just how much our Father is cherished.

Angels exist, and they are real. God, Jesus, and the Holy Spirit are here. The righteous angels made an impactful and memorable realization as I listened to the holy praise. I wanted to remember and memorize their words because the part "Who Was, And Is, And Is To Come" I did not quite understand. I had never heard it before, but it held a massive depth of resolute meaning from how the angels declared. There were other outstanding phrases in chanting joyous proclamations, glorious to hear, as they rang true in the core of my heart.

Jesus was more adept than me at winding His way through the angels. Soon, He was ahead of me and not seen.

Trying to get to Jesus' side, one or another angel was blocking me. At first, I didn't think it was on purpose. Each time I took a step to get through and back to Jesus' side, I wasn't allowed to go in any direction. Angels accomplished this with an action to stand and impede my way a few times, and when one angel stopped me with a spear, I got the correct idea to stay put. He didn't point the spear at me. The spear's staff was on the floor, at the base of the angel's foot, with the angel holding the spear higher on the rod. He straightened his arm so that the spear went out from him and in front of me, preventing my going farther.

Stopping me from moving occurred as the angels were reciting and chanting/singing their praise. Getting the idea, I stayed there in that spot as many tall and large angels moved in much closer to surround me. I was standing in a circle of warrior angels with a foot between us. It felt so good to be cloaked in this way. The angels were at least twenty deep, and I was in the middle as they praised our Father. I felt powerfully accepted and loved.

Their songs of praise lifted me in gloriousness. It was a breathtaking state of dignity and grandeur where nothing else mattered, apart from flowing love to noble and sublime Almighty God. There was an instant transition.

I saw God sitting on His throne. It was just His outline with the rest of Him, a brightest pale yellow light. There was a rainbow, much light, colors, and activity of universes and shooting stars behind the Father on His throne.

Father's outline revealed His glorious long hair and His long robe. He was sitting, leaning slightly to His right with His left foot supported higher on a footstool. He was in the distance with hundreds of thousands of angels in lines before Him. I radiated enhanced love to God by knowing our Creator through how the angels knew and loved Him. Father, after a few moments, also knew I was there and who I was. O, this incredible actualization! Jesus was there too, toward the left. I knew Jesus was looking and taking notice of me and that He was aware of my presence as well. It would seem the same for the hundreds of thousands of angels in the presence of God. I knew with intimacy the unique personalities of Lord Jesus and Father.

The front rows of angels before God were in rows vertically toward Him. Our Father dispatched them as He chose an angel from the heads of the lines. The angel would run fast with enthusiasm to accomplish our Father's bidding. I watched the angels being dispatched in their duties and errands this way for quite a while.

Holy Father's Face

I noticed a man's face in front of me as He appeared slowly, delicately, and closely. I realized who it was and exclaimed with love in my heart, O! It's You! Our Father smiled at me with intimacy, love, kindness, acceptance, and approval. He was cheerful with thick, glorious silver hair that curls with distinct deep waves. I only saw His face, so I don't know what our Father was wearing. His appearance was slightly larger than my regular size but nowhere near His gigantic size on His throne, where He was an outlined yellow light. The angels eagerly waiting for His command were the size of the last joint of His little finger. I can now understand how God loves all sinners and humankind from experiencing His personality and great tenderness. His emanated presence exuded relaxed power and gentleness. I wanted to stroke his hair, but I ceased out of respect, although I felt affectionate. Lord Jesus gave me all! I am richly blessed and grateful for this enduring, glorious, meaningful experience that will never leave me!

I wonder why I didn't die when I saw God's face. Maybe it's because I was in heaven. I don't doubt my physical human body would perish had His presence been experienced here on earth. Beloved reader, I wish I had answers to these incredible open vision mysteries of God.

Two Thrones

The transition back to the enormous room where we entered and heard the angels' chanting was instant. I was still in the center of the many angels. The angels silently walked over to the left of the central aisle, where they lined up in orderly rows. I wished that I could have heard them chant some more. They quietly folded their wings over themselves. They were unseen except for their wings, which were more enormous than usually depicted, covering them completely, including their heads. I walked over to stand by Jesus, who was never far away, even when the angels sang. I knew He was always right there, though I couldn't see Him because of all the towering angels separating us as they praised our Father. Jesus motioned with open–palmed dignity to have me look toward the front,

Lord Jesus: My Father's throne is there.

Jesus displayed with His open left hand the larger throne, straight ahead, at the end of the aisle where we were standing. He revealed the other throne to the left of the larger one with His kindly outstretched arm and opened palm. They were simple, humble thrones without elaborate designs. He gestured with quiet humility,

Lord Jesus: This is my throne.

The infinite expanse of the room had a textured stone floor. It was dark charcoal–colored. The room had indirect lighting that was soft and subdued, with tall and wide columns creating a holy, respectful atmosphere that was lovely, serene, and graceful.

How I was in another area seeing Our Father as a yellow light is not something I have understood because Lord Jesus showed me both of the wooden thrones (with no one on them) in the original room where angels sang their praises. Please forgive my inability to describe these fantastic occurrences accurately.

Lord Jesus gave me the ability to memorize what was happening; many things have remained inexplicable despite this.

Alan, myself, and another would be in this room with wooden thrones. Jesus showed with an elegant gesture to the right of the aisle we were standing in,

Lord Jesus: Behold. This is where you will be.

The empty section to the right of the aisle became filled with human forms. In reality, they were not there. They were transparent, darkly smoke–colored shadows I could see through. They were depictions of what was to be. Looking where Jesus was gesturing, I saw three blank spots in the eighth row from the thrones and five standing places inward from where we stood. Why three empty spaces? My Lord Jesus explained with a discernment download, but I did not keep the voluminous events in the life portrayals of several people. There were so many occurrences and details of people's lives. I feel unworthy not to have been able to keep more of the entire fantastic and enlightening experience.

Gratitude overflows for the many blessings given. It was not for years later, through Bible teachings, that I learned the dead sleep and are not in heaven yet.

I remembered what Jesus showed me. It was a meaningful and kind picture for Him to portray that completely humbles this unworthy servant. He took the time and determination to show me many glorious truths, and I am eternally thankful from the innermost core of my being.

Behold Their Wings

Jesus and I walked toward the angels and we stopped twenty feet from them. The angels were in front of us, praying silently with their folded wings covering them,

Lord Jesus: Behold. Their wings are not white.

I looked at their wings to see they were beige with brown trim on their feathers' tips, having the patterns and likeness of wild birds. Their wings were fascinating and full of glittering sparkles. Jesus gently and patiently urged me,

Lord Jesus: Go and look more closely.

I hesitated for a couple of reasons. Letting go of Jesus' hand was not something I wanted to do. The angels surrounded themselves in their wings, and they were hugely tall, and I didn't want to disturb their worship. However, our Commander of Heaven, Lord of Angels Jesus, coaxed me to go ahead. I let go of His palm and walked up to the angels, but not yet close to them,

Lord Jesus: Go near to them and see their
               wings. They are not white.

Getting a little more nearby, I was thankful to observe there was no disturbance from me and that the Angels were still standing quietly with their wings folded neatly, completely concealing their forms. I was at the edge of their lines. I could see some of the angels' fronts with just the tips of their feet showing, and the other way, I could see them from behind.

My closing in on them occurred as quickly as possible to obey Jesus. They all looked the same to me. I became bolder and walked up to an angel. Standing on the aisle, I randomly selected this angel five rows up from where I stood. He was a few rows away from the sacred thrones of Father and Jesus.

I walked up to the angel and looked at his wings more intently in obedience to our Lord Jesus. I noticed how other wings went far above his head so that I could not see his head, but just feathers that went from top to bottom. Getting right up on his back, I was behind the angel, leaning over and inspecting his wings, with my face six inches away. The beauty of the feathers was astonishing, because each one was exquisite. Not a feather was out of place or ruffled. They were all sleek, new–looking, shiny, alive, and healthful. The loftier feathers' tips had a light wash of pure gold.

I noticed the sparkles. I inspected one of them steadily and intently. The sparkle was an eye! There were sparkly eyes all over his wings. It was the wetness of an eye that caught the light and glittered. They looked like human eyes embedded into the feathers with lighter, shorter wisps of feathers serving as eyelashes. The eyes were resting and not paying attention, listlessly open halfway. While peering at one eye, it opened in awareness to see myself. All the eyes, too many to count, did the same! All those eyes noticed me at once. The eyes blinked in full awareness and caught me, awakened to my presence. What a tremendous startle for both of us as those eyes looked at me, and I looked at them!

The angel turned to face me. It was one swift, robust and military response as he leaped, twisting in midair, landing steadily, his knees bent in a full stride—ready for action. The angel was out of formation and facing me in the aisle. He spread his wings out fully and widely in controlled alarm. He had his sword drawn up into the air, ready to strike. He was inspecting me up and down, poised and unflustered, only moving his eyes as he keenly scrutinized what was out of place among heavenly beings.

I stood, not daring to break eye contact, flinch, breathe or move in case this would provoke an unwanted action. And he was looking straight into my eyes with a severe and stern expression. What a sight he was. The angel was giant and stately, standing poised with fully expanded extensive wings. He looked intent, taking in all elements of me with the suspicion and restraint of a competent soldier. I never looked at myself to determine my attire or my appearance. I can't help to think now, with the Bible's teachings, that it was wretched, worthless rags he saw. Remarkably, the other angels were unaware of what was transpiring and remained shrouded in their beige, brown, and black, wild bird–patterned wings, glittering with eyes.

Jesus Is Commander

Jesus intervened, but I didn't hear any words or conversation. The angel relaxed, straightened, and girded his weapon with quick, heroic prowess. He walked determinedly, quickly, and respectfully over to our Lord and Commander Jesus. Not wanting to intrude on Jesus and the angel, but not wanting to just stand alone over by the other angels, I made my way over to Jesus' right–hand side. I did not take His hand to hold, nor was there any attempt to do so out of respect for not interrupting. He was communicating with the angel as I took my position three feet from His right side, where the angel was in view. Their complete concentration was on each other in telepathic interaction.

The angel had taken off his helmet and held it under his arm. He was full of courage, honor, intelligence, goodness, and the highest values. All this was visible in his shining and charming countenance. He looked to be about thirty–five years old and full of righteous wisdom. His attire was Greek–style armor. He had a brownish–red, short–sleeved tunic under a leather breastplate in matching color of brownish–red. This wonderful angel wore brown leather, open–toed sandals. The sandals crisscrossed up his calves to his knees. The handsome war skirt arrangement of leather straps called a "pteryges" in Greek was finished in brown leather with gold medallions and gold trim for reinforcement at the ends of the leather straps. Interestingly, "Pteruges πτέρυγες" from the Greek word meaning feathers translates to "wings."

> Pteruges (also spelled pteryges, from Greek, meaning feathers) refers to the decorative skirt of leather or fabric strips worn around the waists of Roman and Greek warriors and soldiers
>> From: "Pteruges"
>> http://militaryhistory.fandom.com /wiki/Pteruges
>> (Accessed June 9, 2022)

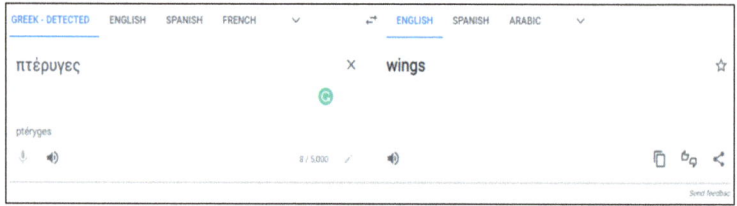

From: Google Translate
https://translate.google.com/
(Accessed April 10, 2022)

I was looking at a magnificent, capable, and seasoned warrior—a victorious hero and champion against Satan and his rebellious army of demon angels, now shamed, fallen, and lost to God. Admiration overflowed to think that this angel speaking to Jesus was one to cast Satan out in defense of heaven, God's righteous character, and God's law.

The angel stood with engrossed concern and loyal obedience toward the Commander of Heaven. His shining and alert countenance, directed toward our Lord, held a serious, principled, and respectful attitude as the Commander of Heaven spoke to him for an extended period. The angel remained steadfast in gaze, assertiveness, and expression in his face and body in front of our Lord. His face was clean-cut with his hair in brunette, neat curls just clearing his shoulders. Plenty of time passed to observe and memorize the angel's appearance as he listened to Commander Jesus Christ.

He focused upward toward Jesus, who was taller. What Commander Jesus was relaying was silent to me. I maintained respect for them in what involved only the Commander of Heaven, Jesus, and the fantastic angel.

Angelic Gaze

Their conversation lasted a long time. The angel acknowledged to Jesus that he understood with a purposeful, single nod. The angel turned toward me, and his demeanor changed to complete ecstasy. He was pleased, welcoming, and appreciative as we looked eye–to–eye. This angel's eyes radiated sparkles with his shining, intelligent, full–of–wisdom, gaze. With complete and utter love, acceptance, and welcoming, he stared into my eyes with his warm smile and memorable glance that I will never forget.

The beaming of his face to mine with such extensive love is indescribable and, truthfully, not of this earth. The honor, the glory, the nobility, and love were profound in what shone from the angel's eyes. There was complete fulfillment, and I blessedly experienced what it is like in heavenly paradise. I felt strongly invigorated with every cell of my being intensely reacting to this angelic love. Without breaking eye contact, he tilted his head to the side for me to notice his neatly–trimmed, 1/2–inch wide strip of beard that trailed along his manly jawline.

The angel's countenance changed into a form that I did not understand. His face morphed. I rapidly noticed he was not so good-looking anymore, and there was an odd smile wherein his cheeks were more prominent and out of proportion. It was startling. Everything was still there in pouring out love, but he had changed his facial features.

I have since learned the cherubim have four faces: Human, Lion, Ox, and Eagle. It was the lion's face. I wish I had known what this change was. Everything was unfamiliar to me. His strange lion's mouth made a quick, peculiar smile with the lion's face, and then he left, walking off in the direction to my right. The cherubim are magnificent, powerful warriors in the service of God. One angel killed 185,000 Assyrian soldiers at once (II Kings 19:35). They do not look like babies with little wings.

I was completely wide–eyed. I asked Jesus what his name was, and he told me it was Daniel. O, Angel Daniel. That's a perfect name. Easy to remember, I thought.

The Heavenly Sanctuary

The transition was instant again. Jesus and I were standing in front of an imposing granite stone building's open rectangular entrance. The structure's shape was a high rectangle. Ornamentation surrounding the edge of the opening was a dark outline carved in the granite. What I saw was gorgeous, simple, strong, and massive construction. Large trees shaded the gigantic structure's front face and the door. The surroundings were quiet, with the fresh leafy vines and bushes making it welcoming.

Lord Jesus: Would you like to go inside and see
                where I work? You can go and see except
                for the last room which is secret.

Sorry to this day, I declined. I imagined an office with a desk and chairs, which didn't appeal to me. Also, that there was something secret made me decide I had just better not. Now my prayer is that Jesus takes the time, if possible, for me to be in open vision again and taken to the Heavenly Sanctuary, if it is His will. I prayed on August 26, 2021, for this vision.

The next day the Holy Spirit moved me to read the book *Maranatha The Lord is Coming* for the devotion that day. August 27th's devotion title is "Study the Subject of the Sanctuary," p.247. I laughed, and I thought about it. I figured to become the most knowledgeable on a subject possible, first, would be necessary to gain the most from the experience of being there at the Sanctuary. It's my hope anyway, and I'll prepare by continuing to study the subject of the Sanctuary most thoroughly!

There are many things I would have asked Jesus if I had some Christian background or knowledge. What was it you wrote on the ground (John 8:1–11)? Has the Sanctuary always existed in heaven? What was the fate of the earthly Ark of the Covenant and its contents? Hopefully, I'll live in heaven, and studying will reveal the many mysteries of God's incredible grand design.

Back From Heaven

We were not in heaven anymore, but I was still in an open vision experience. I knew I was leaving and going back to earth. I didn't want to go back. It was a fast flight through what seemed like the dark abyss alongside the narrow mountain trail we walked on to the city.

Jesus accommodated me when we got back to earth, and we walked and remained together on the property where I was staying in the camper trailer. The birdies followed us again and caroled as they flew intimately nearby, darted up ahead, and waited for Jesus to pass by. He pointed out the landscape on the nearby mountains. The clouds were making alluring darkened shadows of contrast on the hillsides. He explained some people worship the earthly creation when instead they should honor the Creator. My concluding reflection turned to all the cherished people in the world. It would entail a monumental task for all of them to be saved. How could everyone enjoy an experience such as mine was something I inwardly wondered about because it took effort and time? He said with appreciation, confidence, and love,

Lord Jesus: Do not worry. Every person will
              be able to make their choice.

I was thankfully assured that Jesus meant, without exception, each distinct and treasured person. Through discernment, He let me know He was indeed going and that we would see each other in the future. I discerned He would always be near and always be with me—this has proven accurate.

He gave me a picture of Himself stepping onto a train's sideboard, and as it and He were drifting away, Jesus said His last words to me in this open vision that He graciously took the time to provide. He said to me in ecstasy, with His open palm stretched out, waving goodbye, with His loving, brilliant smile I can never forget,

Lord Jesus: Everything you need to know is in the Bible.

Closer in Flowering Accretion

There is no claim at all in being a prophet or anything special, as I am a sinner. There is considerable drive in hoping to be as willing and good a servant as possible. Being in divine, open vision never seemed like it was a dream. Sleep and dreams differ from being awake in an open vision structure. My eyes were open in awareness of physical surroundings at the beginning and the end while in vision. Physical earth receded to where I was not aware of it, starting with being at the sacred cross. Then, back in some physical awareness, I became alert to bow and to lie down on the bed. Physical awareness went away when going through the clouds and stars, on the path, and during the time in heaven. In the end, but still in open vision, I was outside, walking and talking with our Lord Jesus.

What blessings abound in my heart to know Jesus is genuine! These are blessings others can rely on to be true. Being a good Christian is something that I now have a passion for.

I enthusiastically pursued Christianity after the vision and interacting with Jesus. I was a converted Christian from that moment; it felt so good. Learning Christianity and Bible studies took place after another five years. Alan and I were married and placed where Jesus wanted us to be in our small town, attending the charming little country church. Jesus made sure we took part in a church that kept the Sabbath of the seventh day (Saturday), providing for learning the truth we all seek to know.

We were not sure about accepting Prophet Ellen G. White's teachings. We held off on making that decision. I looked her up on the internet to find accusations written about her. I thought that this is certainly how the world would treat a prophet and godly person. We tried to see both sides and make a non–emotional, intelligent decision. After researching more about her, the moment came to make our assessment. This could only come through the ultimate test in studying her writings, which have fascinated us, ever since, with her profound Spirit of Prophecy works. Her works can only have come from being in an open vision and in the presence of Jesus and angels, and her being inspired and guided by the Comforter Holy Spirit.

Drawn to fellow saved Christians, I possessed an eagerness to develop relationships. Attending church was my logical choice to share experiences. In ignorance, I thought everyone had an open vision experience with Jesus and that this was what it was to be saved. My Christian friend explained simply to ask Jesus for salvation, and then I had the glorious rendezvous with Him.

Since being with Jesus, intensely following the Ten Commandments was an enormous passion and held foremost importance in my heart. My desire became ingrained out of what

Jesus went through on the cross and His going over the video file cards with me. I gave sincere promises. According to the Holy Bible, I was grateful to know the actual Ten Commandments correct in numbering and content, because it turns out there are changed versions.

The euphoric vibrations the Holy Spirit imparted have not left in all these years. The tangible vibrations and physical euphoria change a person both inside and outwardly in the material world. Holy Spirit imparted strength to obey and follow newly gained convictions. According to the Law of God, my behaviors—guided by what was written by God's holy finger on two tables of stone given to Moses on Mount Sinai—came from wanting to obey out of love. I now focus on my newfound depth of unfathomable loyalty, adoration, devotion, and commitment in observing the summary of God's law, the Ten Commandments.

How I now laugh at myself for asking Jesus to see God's face, too? No wonder Jesus reacted and wholeheartedly laughed! It was because I took Him literally, not knowing what He was really speaking of when He held out His palms, asking if there was anything more He could do for me.

I now realize Jesus meant anything more than His Sacrifice. He holds His arms and palms in this divine pose, showing the crucifixion scars while asking. Jesus does this as a holy rite. Of course, there is nothing more Jesus Christ, the Son of God, could eternally do for any of us. His glorious and victorious sacrifice gave all of humankind—Eternal Life. Indeed, whatever more is there that Jesus could ever do? Every day, I thank you, my Lord and Protector, Commander of Heaven, Lord of Angels, Son of God, Jesus Christ—for Life.

[16]He hath said, which heard the words of God, and knew the knowledge of the most High, *which* saw the vision of the Almighty, falling into a *trance*, but having his eyes open: (Numbers 24:16)

Miracle Healing~Left Eye

I had an iridocyclectomy surgery performed on my left eye ten months before the heavenly elevation with Jesus. What they described as a birthmark growing inside my eye would have turned into cancer ninety–six percent of the time. The only doctor in the world who executed this type of work performed the eye surgery. He teaches the procedure at Stanford University, California, USA, for future surgeons to develop the ability to do the same surgery. The operation left me with fifteen permanent stitches, kaleidoscope vision (like a geometrical, abstract painting in my left eye), and severe disfigurement that was disturbing for people to see. A considerable section of my eye's white part was now black, pie–shaped, and gaping from the iris to the outer corner.

People could not handle looking at me, so I wore opaque black sunglasses outside and inside public places. Like from the bank, people who remembered me still could not handle it, knowing what was behind those sunglasses. It would take one's breath away to see it. I had arranged some mirrors to get a look. It was horrifying and a shock, making me dizzy. But I had my life, and there was optimism and gratitude from still having my complete eye, when the doctor could have entirely removed it.

Traumatized, crying people in the waiting room sadly had their eye completely removed.

The result of the surgery could not change as far as eyesight went. I was blind in my left eye. I saw some light, but there was so much distortion and blur that any vision was not there. So much so that the big E at the top of the eye chart was unrecognizable. The E fractured into many geometrical shapes that went past the chart into the room. I laughed when first seeing this. I thought the nurses were playing a joke on me.

The surgeon told me permanent stitches held it together "so your eye won't fall apart." The stitches were uncomfortable, and I couldn't tolerate any light in the deep black chasm in my eye's white part. All the time, the stitches caused tearing and dripping down my cheek. I explained it all to Alan. Blessedly for me, Alan was gentle and patient; and it didn't matter to him and he still wanted to marry.

Alan and I were driving back from Vermont to live. He did all the driving, all that way, until the last twenty miles. It was nighttime. He was tired and asked me to drive those last few of the three thousand miles. Not having used a car since the surgery, it was uncertain how well I could handle driving. But how could anything but a yes be the answer to the sweet one who drove the car all that way?

The interstate at this point was three lanes per side. Everything appeared fine until facing oncoming traffic and the headlights from the oncoming cars. This was just about the time I got to full freeway speed. The kaleidoscope vision was so severe that the oncoming vehicles broke up into abstract paintings, which were not definable as vehicles. The geometric parts came clear over the front of our car. It blinded me in this manner and

I could not see at all to drive. I screamed and begged Alan to help me somehow pull over to the side of the road, telling him I was completely blind and could not see where I was driving. For all I knew, I could have been driving off the road into the mountainside. I asked him to please take the wheel and drive from the passenger side to the side of the road. The panic was a frenzy of confusion and alarm. I kept shrieking in terror and asking him to take the wheel while trying to look out the side window to glimpse recognizable lines to be guided by on the road's pavement.

Alan silently prayed without my knowing what he was doing. It was such a surprise that in an instant, the kaleidoscope–like vision was gone. The headlights were round, and the cars looked normal. It was unique and unforgettable. The problem remedied quickly, and it was simply unbelievable that this miracle could happen in a flash. My improved eyesight was a joyous surprise and a gift from God. Still, it was a surprise because I didn't know what had happened, and I couldn't explain it in my mind.

I wasn't aware until later of what had taken place. Alan explained he appealed to Jesus for help. I didn't know that a person prayed to Jesus for healing miracles. I thought they just happened at Lord Jesus' will.

I asked Alan why he didn't respond to my screams. How come he didn't take the wheel from the passenger side and guide the car down the freeway? His response was a blessed, simple one. He said that he was praying to our Lord and Savior Jesus. May we ring bells for our Father's abundant mercies and Alan's extraordinary faith in making the correct choice.

Miracle Healing~Left Eye (Completed)

Alan was kind and understanding about the struggles with my problem eye. Any light hurt, making tears, and constant tearing was also from irritable, permanent stitches. I was getting ready to wear a pirate patch to keep the light out. Not exactly a fashionable choice for a lady, but maybe a necessary step to take. One morning, out of compassion, Alan said, "Come over here." He cupped his palm over my left eye. He held me warmly as we embraced. Instantly, I felt the healing. It felt so good. Physically, it was soothing with much comfort. It was immediate relief of on–going sharp pain, plus there was something else I felt as though my eye was changing. I felt an easing massage inside my eye. It felt fantastic. He held me this way for a few minutes while he prayed. I will never forget being held by him, just standing together in the living room. Alan, this wondrous man, was so happy when he stopped, looked, and openly satisfied with the accomplishment in answer to his sweet, silent, and simple prayer. I didn't know he was praying for healing because I wasn't used to his praying silently, and I mostly thought we were just enjoying some hugging.

Alan continued a healing prayer at night (aside from regular daily worship) until my eye healed entirely. It was a slow mending that took one week. Alan kept checking my eye here and there. He looked me over, cocking his head from the side, and informed me with a smile that my eye was regular. All this time and long afterward, I never looked because of the trauma of seeing it before. I did not know what to think, but he was happy about having everything normal with my eye. I delightedly and gratefully accepted. Alan said that it was not he who healed me, but Jesus. Today, my eye is still completely normal. There is no disfigurement, and my eye has a round iris, and the rest of the eyeball is the usual white.

Sometime later, seeking to have the stitches removed, I discovered I needed cataract surgery for both eyes. I kept telling the doctors and assistants that I used to have severe disfigurement from a previous surgery and that my eye miraculously healed. They needed to know the circumstances and the actual medical history, and I asked them to please remove the fifteen stitches that were still there. Whenever speaking this way, the medical staff and doctors would straight away leave the room, saying nothing. But after getting the medical records from the physician who performed the surgery, the medical personnel realized what I was saying was true. There was no way my eye could ever have healed, and it was never meant to, from that surgery. Doctors cannot officially recognize miracle cures; however, a doctor admitted, after a long conversation, that it was sure there had been some manipulation.

During subsequent visits for my husband, Zach (Alan had expired, and I remarried.), indirectly but unmistakably, a doctor used the word "miracle" a few times as their look directly referenced my left eye. It strengthened Christian hope for those who knew and could not refute the hard evidence. Though it was an earnest effort for this doctor to believe and accept, ultimately, they did, and they told me. I am grateful to Jesus and blessed to have my complete eye with good, functioning eyesight, instead of frightening people when they see me coming.

[27]Behold, I *am* the Lord, the God of all flesh:
is there any thing too hard for me?
(Jeremiah 32:27)

Is there no thing He cannot do?
Angel Daniel (to Snowye)

Miracle Healing~Malignant Breast Cancer

I noticed a lump in my breast and had a mammogram to see what it was. The mammogram led to a biopsy to test for cancer. The pathology report from the biopsy determined it was invasive ductal carcinoma, as did the follow–up MRI. This is aggressive breast cancer that the doctors gave seven months for me to live if left untreated. Treatment meant mastectomy surgery, chemotherapy, and radiation. All three treatments were medicine I just did not wish to go through because of all the side effects, which do not promote a good quality of life.

Alternative medicine in other countries using dendritic cell therapy is much more successful if the patient has not had chemotherapy and radiation, which severely damages the immune system. Dendritic cell therapy is a last resort in America after surgery/chemotherapy/radiation. It uses a person's unique white blood cells customized and proliferated to attack the malignancy, no matter where the cancer cells are in the body.

The dendritic cell treatment is expensive. Zach and I were waiting to sell our home for the funds to accomplish dendritic cell technology offered in Mexico.

My ardent, dear husband Zach and I held sadness, and we felt troubled. We realized how stressed we were at the thought of an invasive removal of my complete breast (possibly both) and my potential death. An ominous pall weighed on both of us as we saw our lives changing forever.

The stress was enormous. We went to lie on our bed, and we cuddled for comfort. Zach and I prayed for help with our crisis. We prayed for divine healing for my breast and strength to cope with the abrupt changes that were inserted into our still new life together.

Zach held his hand over the area with his fingers cupped lightly on the protruding malignant tumor. We confessed our sins and asked for forgiveness in heartfelt repentance. Zach and I took turns praying aloud and claimed many of God's promises. I'm so grateful for Zach's knowledge of God's word, His promises, and how to pray. We believed in His promises because the Father cannot lie as He is righteous, and it isn't a part of His character to tell any untruths, ever.

We first acknowledged our Father's greatness and His being full of mercy and grace. We counted our blessings and realized his great love and creation of the world and humanity. We thanked Him for being who He is and His conception of Zach and myself and that we hoped to be worthy children of His.

It was a humble appeal as we surrendered our hearts to our merciful Creator and Redeemer, expressing our sincere sentiments about our entire lives. At the end of our supplication for curing my breast cancer, Zach concluded by asking that the healing only take place should it be God's will. Just as Zach said, "will," it happened!

At that moment, Lord Jesus and Angel Daniel blessed me with an open vision. I heard a loud pop sound, much like when the pressure releases from a jar's lid when first opening it or pulling a cork from a bottle. I saw Zach's fingers depress as the tumor collapsed under his fingers. The total experience was stunning, and I remained silent, along with Zach's silence. Usually, the end of our prayer would conclude with Zach saying, "Thank you for hearing our prayer, in precious Jesus' name. Amen." But not this time. Instead, I was mulling over what had happened and waiting for Zach to close the devotion. I asked Zach if he heard what I heard and saw what I saw, but Zach kept his silence. I wondered if there was anything heard or seen by him. Zach then explained a few moments later that he was taking it all in from his particular point of view. He wanted to solidify and keep the memory of his specific realization of what had just happened. Several days later, he told me his experience, confirming it was the same as mine.

We were enlightened more than three years ago, since September 16, 2019, with the holy miracle of taking cancer from my breast and body. I have no symptoms of cancer illness or demise with destroyed tissue and ulcers that should be had by now from having cancer, as the doctors said. We prayed using the following promises in the Holy Bible from the innermost part of our hearts and souls.

> ^{2}In hope of eternal life, which God, that cannot lie, promised before the world began;
> (Titus 1:2)

> ^{18}Come now, and let us reason together, saith the Lord: though your sins be as scarlet, they shall be as white as snow; though they be red like crimson, they shall be as wool.
> (Isaiah 1:18)

[2]Ye lust, and have not: ye kill, and desire to have, and cannot obtain: ye fight and war, yet ye have not, because ye ask not.
(James 4:2)

[22]And all things, whatsoever ye shall ask in prayer, believing, ye shall receive
(Matthew 21:22)

[9]And I say unto you, Ask, and it shall be given you; seek, and ye shall find; knock, and it shall be opened unto you.
(Luke 11:9)

[10]Bring ye all the tithes into the storehouse, that there may be meat in mine house, and prove me now herewith, saith the LORD of hosts, if I will not open you the windows of heaven, and pour you out a blessing, that there shall not be room enough to receive it.
(Malachi 3:10)

[24]And it shall come to pass, that before they call, I will answer; and while they are yet speaking, I will hear.
(Isaiah 65:24)

[5]Every word of God is pure: he is a shield unto them that put their trust in him.
(Proverbs 30:5)

[35]And Jesus went about all the cities and villages, teaching in their synagogues, and preaching the gospel of the kingdom, and healing every sickness and every disease among the people.
(Matthew 9:35)

Before going to sleep, Zach kneels by the bed on my side in the evenings. He holds my hand and prays to Our Lord in thankfulness for what occurred in a miracle, saving my life, saving our lives together.

There are other healings not included here. These are a couple of the extraordinary ones proven with medical records.

Zach and I, seized with wonder and gratefulness, realize how fortunate we are. We both ponder and ask why. Our Father, Jesus, Holy Spirit, and Angels are real, alive, and active, contrary to popular opinion in these times of last–day events until the close of this world. Satan's desire utterly to destroy all humankind is driven by his abominable idea of—death forever. The Holy Bible is full of God's promises for mending, salvation and—life forever.

Jesus Still Guides Me

I was lying down, resting with my eyes open. Jesus' beautiful face appeared up near the ceiling as if he came through clouds.

Lord Jesus: In my name, all issues.

I heard His words as I was dreaming of a new home, while exercising on the strength/cardio/stretch device:

Lord Jesus: Stop striving for things of the
world, and you will have it all.

Carillon of An Angel

Angel Daniel in My Worldly Life

Holy Spirit was present, and open vision came on me as I rested in bed. He was dressed in the finest cream–colored attire. Intricately worked design in pure gold filigree enhanced the gorgeous Greek–style armor. It was finely done, ornamental gold openwork for the helmet. The breastplate was tasteful, finely–worked, with intricate gold filigree designs over creamy–colored white, impeccably–fitted, soft leather. The gold metalwork was the same gorgeously done filigree on the shining sword's hilt with a silver handle. Gold filigree design was elaborately placed on the finely made solid gold shield. The shin coverings he was wearing matched with gold metalwork filigree on cream–colored leather. The gold metalwork and all the metals were not imitation. It was pure gold metal—gleaming, subtle, rich, and beautifully lustrous.

Angel Daniel kneeled on one knee. He took his right hand, fingers closed on the sword, kissed his closed, fisted hand, and then slowly and deliberately, with serious strength in nobility, placed his fist with the solemn kiss onto my left shoulder. It was a noble act with a fulfilling purpose. It was a meaningful and somber rite with tremendous respect and honor that was elegantly given.

Since Angel Daniel's formal sacrament, I was more conscious of his nearness. I am blessed and humbled that he took the time for this ceremonial rite. I accepted and recognized his unique attention and closeness. He makes his presence known here and there with an audibly heard word or phrase and physical earthly manipulations when they are needed. There is gratitude, caring, and love felt both ways between us. Harmonious communion and admiration in what a wondrous and incredible creation of our Father's he was, resulted in Angel Daniel's humble reply,

Angel Daniel: Man is higher.

Fully committed, Angel Daniel and I are much like a team. He is my bedrock, having saved my life, comforted me, and spoken needed information to me. Indeed, he knows all about me already. He shares with me. My Angel Daniel is helping me to write *Carillon* with gentle suggestions. Possibly in a future book, I will write more about our conversations.

sacrament [sak-ruh-muhnt]
noun

1. | ...
5. | a sign, token, or symbol.
6. | an oath; solemn pledge.

> From: Sacrament Definition Meaning
> Dictionary.com
> https://www.dictionary.com/browse/
> sacrament
> (Accessed June 9, 2022)

Consolation in An Angel's Wings

There was a problematic substructure with a person I was dealing with where it was ongoing, stressful, and tiresome. I needed help to find resolve and relief. Wondering what I could do and prayerfully seeking a cordial conclusion, I heard my angel's strong words of support. I was in open vision with him standing behind me. He shrouded his wings entirely over me, so they came clear to the front. Cocooned inside his fantastic and large feathered wings, we were close, with my back to him but not touching. My angel's love and protection were consoling, full of peace, and comforting. He conveyed a tremendous feeling of solace, serenity, contentment, and strength.

Angel Daniel: I am going to take care of this, right now!

The vision was of his leaving to take care of the complete state of affairs. I also knew nothing would stop this. The situation would draw to a close. Angel Daniel remedied the entire case brought about by nothing but devils. He whispered to me a little later that he would have to be their angel, as well. He said it with such kindness and tenderness. Of course, it was okay with me! He acted with upliftment on their behalf using miracles. Angel Daniel influenced a resolve with their moving from the area.

When Jesus handles interpersonal difficulties, the results are suitable for everyone involved. This is true, without exception, when leaving all in Jesus' thoroughly competent and dedicated hands. It is a state of surrender, and it involves praying to God for all issues in Jesus' name.

Blessings abound for me, having the experience and realization of the purpose of ultimate consolation in my Angel Daniel's winged embrace.

> If we expect our own prayers to be heard we must forgive others in the same manner and to the same extent as we hope to be forgiven.
> White, Ellen G.
> *Steps to Christ* (1982), p. 97

Angel Forums

Angels conduct forums in heaven. They're a physical forum, unlike an internet one where we type the statements and press the enter key to post. It was a privilege for me to be in vision for a few moments while two of them were held on my behalf.

The forum platform is an outdoor, open–air, rectangular pavilion outlined by tall columns set on the same foundation used for walking. It was a concrete or stone foundation. The ornate order of the columns' capitals (Ionic, Doric, or Corinthian) was a different order from what I knew while I inspected and admired them. The setting was ancient, with patina on the stone, but there was no debris or any disrepair. Along one side, there were tables with water fountains to enjoy. The tables covered in white linen with a fountain nearby were unwrinkled and immaculate. The angels filled their ornately carved silver chalices, taken from the tables, and drank from the fountain flow. It was crystal clear, life–giving water flowing from the fountain.

Attractive, brightly–flowered vines with lush, deep green leaves climbed the columns and collected at the top, wildly cascading back down in a beautiful display. Vines also went column–column at the top and lushly draped from there. Looking through the columns to the outside was a gorgeous countryside landscape, mostly deep green with trees sumptuous with colorful and large flowers. There were rolling hills and mountains covered in deep green bushes and tall trees, providing breaths and sighs of ecstasy in the peaceful distance.

Angel Daniel stood at one end of the garden pavilion and had asked a question. Angels who were interested in participating came from throughout heaven's vast expanse. There were hundreds of them attending. They came to brainstorm and come up with the best course of action to accomplish an answer to Angel Daniel's question. This is one way angels voluntarily come together to help achieve God's will toward our best outcomes, as Jesus commands.

Angels walked back and forth in the pavilion in calm, serious, slow strides as they contemplated a solution. The angels strolled, mingled, and passed one another. If a thought came to mind, they would promptly stop and present it to a random and nearby angel. They might converse a bit, more might join in, and then they would continue, mingling, expressing, and deliberating as they thoughtfully strode along the pavilion. The promenading and small groups would grow into larger groups and then disperse, contemplating the best outcomes and planned actions to take for an improved situation. Glorious are they in their sanctified work for the benefit of humankind.

At some point, all would come to a best plan and consensus. The angels then presented their final findings for the solution to the angel who had asked—in this case, Angel Daniel. It might take hundreds or more of the angels taking part in executing a particular role for the chosen solution.

I saw that angels diligently work together toward our best conclusions for any situation discussed. They are watching with tremendous interest and love. Angels possess the ability to step in where most needed to change our courses toward spending eternal life in heaven. The Father assigns this ardent, serious, and intense work which is commanded by beloved Jesus toward addressing the crisis currently being played out on earth between good and evil.

Angels wield unbelievable power and the ability to rectify any part of our lives needed. Rectification is not about granting our selfish and meaningless wishes. According to our Father's will, it is work accomplished that results in our soul's development to live eternally in heaven. The precise work considers aspects that warrant close internal inspection of our subtler side. I saw in heaven how the angels line up by the hundreds of thousands in front of our Father, awaiting His dispatch to run and immediately accomplish the all–merciful Creator's commands toward our best ends. The affairs of every one of us human beings are blessed this way, and most of us don't even know it.

Our fiercest determination should be to develop a Christ–like character as depicted in the Bible regarding the Fruit of the spirit (Galatians 5:22–23). Think on the nine attributes of noble character, keeping them in our thoughts and acting accordingly. This allows the halo of heaven to shine through us into this dark world. In this state, we become surrendered vessels that heavenly hearts can work through. What untold blessings of mystery this brings!

Where An Angel Walked

Prophet Ellen G. White wrote about what will come for humankind to face in these perilous and troublesome end times. In the quote below, Sister White describes the protection arranged by angels. I questioned Jesus during prayer if this would be actual physical protection in this context. Maybe protection would be placement into the Comforter Holy Spirit's select state of being. Possibly this way, it wouldn't matter if affliction and emotional torment were at hand, and in this uplifted state, they could endure the intolerable. I was thinking about the Reformation Martyrs. If they genuinely felt the torturous fiery flames from being burned on a pyre of wood, they could never be singing and reciting Bible verses. Could they?

> Some are assailed in their flight from the cities and villages; but the swords raised against them break and fall powerless as a straw. Others are defended by angels in the form of men of war.
> White, Ellen G.
> *The Great Controversy*, p. 631

Heartfelt Prayer

I questioned if it would be actual physical protection in the time of trouble, according to the prophet's words, or if protection were another way. I asked this of God, Jesus, and my Angel Daniel. I asked God for permission if it was His will, and I asked for it to be permitted. I asked Jesus as Commander of my angel that it only happen if Lord Jesus' goals could still accomplish with Angel Daniel's departure; if this would please be only with Jesus' permission. I asked for my Angel Daniel to spend personal time away from his duties. This was only if:

1. His duties remained productive despite his possible departure.
2. Should my dear Angel Daniel decide to accommodate, this would only be because he was willing, not my will.

I petitioned that Angel Daniel please come to earth so that I could see him. It would show me it was actual physical protection angels can provide in times of trouble, such as man has never known.

I knew angels visited Abraham and visited men and women other times in the Bible. There was confidence in the possibility that my angel could visit earth, should this be the answer to my request? I told my husband, Alan, about the wish should he be present if the decision was for Angel Daniel to make the journey to earth.

The Wonderful Place

There was a plan with my husband (Alan) on our exit of the big box store. I wanted to walk across the parking lot in the mild, pleasant weather rather than ride to the nearby fabric store. Alan agreed to take the groceries in the shopping cart, put them into the truck, and then meet at the fabric store. He went to get the car and bring it up to the entrance/exit to load the cart from there. It was not our usual shopping routine, where we simply took the purchases out to the parking lot. I felt walking in the warm dusk and feeling the softness of the air would be a delight. It was so pleasant, quiet, and peaceful. The store's boisterousness was gone because people were home having dinner during this time of the evening, just before darkness sets in.

I called it the pat–down. There was even a cyclone fence to walk along to exit the store. You get in line with your receipt in hand, and the employee compares the items in your shopping cart with your receipt before you may exit.

Holy Spirit

It was nice to be only myself with no one in line walking toward the exit–checker. Then, the Holy Spirit came upon me more intensely. Thank you, Holy Spirit, Jesus, and God, for the higher than usual euphoric elation. I was so uplifted with love and appreciated all existence. I enjoyed being able to shop, walk, to push a cart. Life was so good. There were no complaints. Holy Spirit imparted a distinct physical euphoria with mental/emotional fulfillment. I asked why, but there was no answer, and believe me, it didn't matter at all.

Approach from Afar

Stepping outside with the shopping cart to wait for Alan, I noticed a person who was way out in the parking lot. He captured my attention as he was deliberately walking straight toward me, his eyes fixed on mine from way out there. It was like a friend who knew me, but I wasn't so sure I knew him. I gestured with my flattened hand to my chest, saying, "me?" His response was unmistakable. His pace was confident and more deliberate as an immediate answer. Convinced he was indeed approaching me for some unknown reason amazed me.

He wasn't far away when my husband came back from the truck. Alan asked me, "Do you want me to take the cart now?" I was standing and staring, not able to speak. I said no because I wanted him to stay there. But not capable of explaining why, it was so Alan would notice this person approaching me; he asked me again about taking the cart. Alan took charge and went away with the shopping cart while I was still trying to ask him to stay. I had my hand on the front edge of the shopping cart as Alan took it. My fingers and arm were lifeless and dropped to my side when the shopping cart separated from me. I still could not speak physically. I wanted Alan to stay there because an unknown man zeroed in and was walking up to me. But Alan was already taking the shopping cart to load into the truck. It was in a spot not for parking and was marked yellow for loading and unloading only; therefore, Alan was in a hurry.

I stood there. Angel Daniel approached me and stood lovingly, with only a foot between us. He was tall and well–proportioned on the slim side. Angel Daniel must have been six feet, five inches in height. He was casually, neatly, and elegantly dressed in tan slacks and a lightweight brown and cream–colored plaid shirt with casual leather shoes. His attire was the rustic and tasteful Ralph Lauren style. Angel Daniel looked terrific, and he blended in. But I didn't know who he was.

The pleasantly conservative way he dressed would draw no one's attention. My Angel was so handsome, and the heavenly love emanated intensely from his shining and glittering brown eyes. Angels are love. The intense love is captivating so that nothing else matters. However, I wasn't aware that it was Angel Daniel. The love perplexed me. It was pouring out from what I thought to be a stranger. However, standing there and being loved was enjoyable. I wondered if I was familiar with him from somewhere I couldn't remember, even though I was trying. He was beaming brightly with his abounding smile. Then he smiled more broadly and cocked his face at an angle to the side, showing his jawline so I would notice it. Eye contact wasn't broken during this gesture as he continued smiling with joy glistening in his eyes. I saw his neatly trimmed, 1/2–inch wide strip of beard that outlined his entire jaw.

Daniel! So wonderful to see you! Immediately, I memorized all features of his face—his hair, eyes, cheeks, mouth, teeth, and lips. A talented person who is adequately patient with the descriptions could draw it. It is the same as what I remember of Father's and Lord Jesus' facial features.

Communication was with no physically spoken words when I said "Daniel! It's so good to see you!" with elated, though delayed, recognition. My Angel Daniel was joyful to let me know he was there. He was pouring out intense love, just like he did when looking at me in heaven. I was so grateful, humbled, and amazed. He turned, walking away to the right, as I just stood there and watched him, wishing he were staying. My angel got into the entrance check–your–card line with a couple of people ahead.

The same episode happened as it did in heaven. His face transformed, the lion was there, and he gave the same quick, peculiar smile on the lion's face. This time, more detail was being taken in and committed to memory. I could see Angel Daniel's complete form because of the increased distance between us, wherein heaven he was closer.

> ## Meaningfulness
>
> And impact truly overflowed for me when I read the book of Ezekiel in the Bible. Prophet Ezekiel saw what I saw!
>
> ———❖———
>
> [15]Now as I beheld the living creatures, behold one wheel upon the earth by the living creatures, with his four faces. (Ezekiel 1:15)

His legs looked oddly thin. Paying more attention, I saw his legs were a blur when he took steps forward. When he stopped walking, his legs were a lion's back legs, paws, etc.

The blurring shape made the appearance of a wheel and was because of seeing all his four forms' hind legs taking steps simultaneously when he walked. Prophet Ezekiel was right "… as it were a wheel in the middle of a wheel," (Ezekiel 1:16) because each of the eight legs made its round blur.

When he stopped at the entrance checker, I noticed his legs and feet were the hind legs and hooves of the ox. I didn't see Angel Daniel's heavenly wings as I did in heaven. That would have been a spectacular and welcome sight. Those countless eyes embedded in his shiny, wild bird patterned feathers are beautiful. Angel Daniel looked at and spoke to the entrance checker for a moment. I wondered, did he have the card? He entered the store and walked inside toward the shopping aisles. There was no one to be seen. Angel Daniel disappeared, walking through an electric and invisible portal. It sizzled electrically blue on his edges as he walked through it.

I broke down later, crying with gratitude for a very long time, sitting in the truck in the parking lot with Alan. I sing praises in gratefulness to our Father, Jesus, and the Holy Spirit. Gratefulness is flourishing for Angel Daniel, letting me know he was close. He let me be sure he was near and would protect me physically and in all ways possible. Having this blessed message tells me Jesus is coming soon. There is just no mistaking Angel Daniel in seeing his beard trailing his jawline and his lion's face. Gratefulness and adoration flow to our magnificent God, Jesus, and Comforter Holy Spirit for their devotion in answering my request. I am completely blessed with God's unfathomable mystery.

I ponder and contemplate a lot on this blessed gift of experiencing my Angel Daniel here on our earth. Angel Daniel's continued rejoicing and jubilance as he willingly and faithfully performs many duties for our Father and Jesus is what I pray for. Angel Daniel told me a little later that if an angel wants to pick you up and carry you, it's best not to hold on to their neck or any part of the angel. We should cross our arms in front of our chest to be carried in this manner—whether we're in an angel's arms on the ground running or held in their arms while flying.

I ask myself about my capabilities. What if God, Jesus, or Angel Daniel needed my help from an attack? What would I do for them? How binding are my convictions and my love? The fact is, they are being attacked. They need our help right now. Making correct choices to obey God's law and not accepting the evil one is how we accomplish this help. It provides the needed support in the planned abundant action of redemption consummated by

Jesus' sacrifice, giving us eternal and real life. Keeping God's law shows our recognition of His true nature. It's showing allegiance to, and being on the side of, the zealous Creator of ourselves and the universes. It is one way we help the fight in this great controversy on earth between good and evil.

Without exception, when going to the big box store, I asked Alan, "Would you like to walk where an angel walked?" Alan knew about Angel Daniel's visit and joyfully heard this when we went to the store. We made the many angel steps in the entrance area. I remembered where the electric portal was and looked for some evidence of it. We would stand where Angel Daniel stood. We would walk where an angel walked.

> [10]As for the likeness of their faces, they four had the face of a man, and the face of a lion, on the right side: and they four had the face of an ox on the left side; they four also had the face of an eagle.
> (Ezekiel 1:10)

> [17]When they went, they went upon their four sides: and they turned not when they went.
> (Ezekiel 1:17)

> [12]And their whole body, and their backs, and their hands, and their wings, and the wheels, were full of eyes round about, even the wheels that they four had.
> (Ezekiel 10:12)

10

Invitation's Gateway

Lying awake in my bed, I had not yet fallen asleep, and it was well into the early morning hours. I often would contemplate fondly on the open vision with Jesus and talk with Him and Angel Daniel to gain insight into our world and what role I could serve. This night was serene and loving, with Alan asleep beside me. Emotion in my musings overcame me; I had tears running down from the outer corners of my eyes. I was grateful for many beautiful understandings giving me security in what to expect for my future and reasons for what goes on in our world today.

My first awareness was a golden light filling the bedroom. Then I saw golden angels flying above our bed, back and forth, throughout the room. They were in golden robes, had golden wings, and were golden sparkly all over. Engrossed with the beauty of the display, I was still with tears running from the corners of my eyes, with tremendous, powerful love in my heart.

The sparkly golden angels flew in and out above the bed into what seemed like a sky above. Noticing this and hoping they weren't leaving, I saw in its entirety this lovely event, lasting for a long time, captivating me with its splendorous beauty.

Alan woke up for a night call; he looked at the flying golden angels' activity. There must have been fifty flying nearby, in and out of the opening. Farther away, deeper into the portal, it looked like a night sky with twinkling stars. They were flying around in this deeper area, too. I asked Alan what he saw. He said he saw golden angels flying all over the room. He came back to bed and fell to sleep right away. I kept watching, rejoicing in my heart, with tears over its beauty. It was bliss the angels exuded. They were happy and giving, flying in pretty twirls and arcs with their graceful wings as they went up and came back again, others taking their places in sweet chaotic expressions of loveliness.

I noticed the portal. Round, its boundaries were swirling, active, and rolling clouds that extended past the edges of the bed as I lay there looking up. Golden angels were still flying in, out, and above. Many were motionless, not flying but peering over the edge of the opening. I was stunned that they were all looking at me. How come, and what could I do for them?

Then I saw my sweet Angel Daniel. As I looked up, he was over to the left of the circular portal, peering at me over the actively rolling cloudy edge. I was so happy to see him! He took his hand, reached through the opening, and made a beckoning motion. He was saying with this motion to come here. My telepathic reply was, "go there, with you and all the angels?" Breathlessness at the thought of it barely allowed me to think.

Yes, the portal opening was about me going through it and not returning. Should I have? Only a couple of months later was when Alan died. I wanted to go into the portal, conveying this to Angel Daniel and all the angels in attendance, with their glorious display so indescribable. But I said no because I had better obey our Father. I looked over to Alan, gently sleeping, and felt compelled to stay, minding our Father ("… stay with Alan or you will regret it all the days of your life!"). My thoughts were Alan shouldn't be alone. I would avoid having him go through grief, and that he needed me. But mostly, I wanted to obey our Father, and this I communicated to Angel Daniel. He smiled. There were good feelings of appreciation, love, and kindness. At that very moment, the portal and all the activity ended. It quickly closed from its outer edges to the center of what used to be the portal door. Schoop, all gone.

I would have many questions, especially if I went. Would my body remain (but lifeless) when Alan woke up in the morning? Or would I have gone simply and completely disappear like others (Not to compare myself!)? Did Angel Daniel prepare it all for me? I think yes, and now I realize this would never have occurred without the approval of Our Father God and Lord Jesus, with the participation of the Holy Spirit providing the power to make it all happen.

I have no bad feelings about not going. Only the astonishment that a gorgeous portal opened and feeling special, cared for, and humbled that Angel Daniel's and so many other angels' efforts made it possible. This unworthy person did not deserve such consideration and kindness. My life is good because heavenly hearts watch over me. Also, at Jesus' exclamation, I married another wonderful Christian man, Zach. He absolutely stands for what is right though the heavens fall. I am blessed with another exquisite gift from God in Zach, the love between us given by God, that neither of us ever knew could exist.

O, I thank you dear Jesus for these humbling and mysterious experiences in my life!

> The greatest want of the world is the want of men—men who will not be bought or sold, men who in their inmost souls are true and honest, men who do not fear to call sin by its right name, men whose conscience is as true to duty as the needle to the pole, men who will stand for the right though the heavens fall.
> White, Ellen G.
> *Education*, p. 57

Angel Food Diet

Despite healings, I have enduring issues that type 2 diabetes causes, like too many others. The last statistic said one in three people now have it, adults and children alike. That's one–third! I was doing adequately well addressing it with diet, exercise, ketosis, GKI, with no medications to pursue a cure. Adequately well, until Zach's and my second bout with pestilence nineteen's spike protein cobra venom attack. It lasted forty days, as did the first stretch. If we had known what the issue entailed, we could have made our illness shortened. We didn't even know what it was the first time, as it wasn't named and discussed in the news media yet. Angel Daniel expressed we were to have the resistance, so the allowed condition endured. This second time, it must have been from picking up the poison again. Pestilence after Pestilence… However, now we know what to do to avoid getting it (quercetin combo with vitamins c, d, zinc, bromelain) and how to treat most new pestilence infection issues it leaves with people.

It turns out that there's an aftermath to having endured pestilence nineteen. Hair falling out, diabetes ("covid–induced diabetes"), shingles, cancer, and many other serious ailments caused or intensified by having cobra venom plague nineteen. The pestilence extremely exacerbated type 2 diabetes for both of us. Zach was now having glucose readings of a person with full–blown diabetes when he was normal before. My glucose numbers soared to over 300 and would not come down, no matter what I ate. There were heart palpitations, dizziness, fainting, and my blood pressure was severely high on top of it. I felt I was in danger. Fortunately for Zach, his blood sugar readings have returned to normal after working on it with his diet.

Mine remained desperately high. During Zach's and my morning prayer, sweet warrior Angel Daniel began letting me know what to do. It was how to eat and bring down blood pressure. I also had sharp nerve pain from shingles turning inward, caused by pestilence nineteen. I took curcumin for this and am not afflicted with it anymore.

It was a lovely two–way conversation with my Angel Daniel. He would let me know an item, and I would ask if it was okay to add this or that, and the answer was always yes.

Zach and I plan to pray for the healing of diabetes and any other afflictions we may have. Our mindset is that sometimes Father and Jesus may want to see something in our efforts first. For instance, I am indoors a lot and don't get the sunshine and fresh air I should. I don't want to ask for healing unless I am doing all I can on my part first to be healthy with the eight laws of health.

The Angel Food Diet doesn't contain manna or anything special—I just like to call it that. Unfortunately, I cannot provide it here because I'm not a doctor. I will say that the diet calls for adding a salad to every meal (including breakfast), with a dressing of mayonnaise, fresh garlic and lemon juice being the only salad dressing used.

However, it worked very well. In two days, my blood pressure was normal, astoundingly, on the low healthy side that I hadn't seen in decades. It has been low like this ever since. Blood sugar readings have dropped from 316 mg/dL (American) to 120–130 mg/dL. It is dropping steadily around 20–40 points daily, and I'll be happy when it is at a steady level of 90 mg/dL. Moderate to High ketosis GKI (Glucose Ketone Index) has been the result for all this time. With the addition of intermittent fasting and slow burn exercise, this ketosis level should end and cure diabetes type 2 after approximately three months.

During these three months, I'll be soul–searching for any lack of doing the right things for my health and well–being and preparing for the close of probation. Then, Zach and I will pray for healing, going boldly in our hearts before the throne.

Gentle Alan

12

A Good Christian Man, Alan

Today, I have completed *Carillon* short of additional edits and a section in miracle healings. This is an additional part and chapter in this writing. It needed to be added because my dear, sweet husband, Alan, went to sleep six days ago. His departure was sudden and unexpected. The entire situation in God's grace was full of mercy in so many ways for Alan and me. Professionals said there was no suffering, and it was peaceful. It was the same as I saw, going downstairs in our home, after several angels came into my sleep telling me Alan was with me no more.

Alan was one whose prayers also were heard—and answered. Like Zach's, Alan's were beautiful, enduring observances I have had the privilege of attending. I was happy for our Christian home that Alan sweetly and regularly cultivated.

God gave Alan as a gift to me for a short time. Our Father only loaned Alan to me because our Father gave Alan his breath of life. God wanted Alan to return, and God safely protects and remembers Alan because he sleeps and knows nothing for now. This will be until that Great Day when Alan will put on incorruptible and immortal to live in his heavenly home of love, eternally. The hope is that I will be there to see him and my king, Lord Jesus. I want not to be ashamed when I stand before Jesus as much as possible. I work diligently toward being the best I can be, on all levels, for that Great Day.

Alan's conversations and life were about God and our dear Jesus. A Book of Remembrance records those often speaking to one another of God. It must be that Alan is recorded in the Book of Remembrance because he loved our Father, Jesus, and the Holy Spirit and often spoke of them with a substantial depth of closeness and love.

[15]And now we call the proud happy; yea, they that work wickedness are set up; yea, they that tempt God are even delivered. [16] Then they that feared the LORD spake often one to another: and the LORD hearkened, and heard it, and a book of remembrance was written before him for them that feared the LORD, and that thought upon his name. [17] And they shall be mine, saith the LORD of hosts, in that day when I make up my jewels; and I will spare them, as a man spareth his own son that serveth him.
(Malachi 3:15–17)

Good Life

Our marriage was happy and gratifying. Alan was living the life he wanted with celebration. Jesus has my prolific gratitude for the blessings given. We lived in a small, conservative town. We experienced simple people and relationships. Alan and I pursued fellowship, Bible study, and church with vigor and warmth.

Alan loved providing all he could to others. He was truly selfless, meek, and humble. Many times, others influenced by the evil one made a mockery of him in what they thought was a perception of weakness. Had they only known the truth? It takes a healthy, sane, secure, and kind person to be selfless, gentle, and humble. Maybe it takes the same to be a healer and seer of the future.

Alan was a strong and protective man, counted on for what he needed to do as a man. He protected me physically against any danger in a heartbeat.

Alan served on the church board and was reliable to shovel snow at the church and community services. He shoveled walks and sidewalks for the neighbors before they woke up. A man walked for miles to pick up his food at community services. Alan drove this man home to have all of his food and not run out during the month because he couldn't carry it all.

Alan accomplished these kindnesses with unmistakable enthusiasm and sincere, gentle caring. Many remedies in healing others in ways they did not know took place. Alan was about love. He was about nurturing, not only physically, but spiritually. I am thankful to God for having the privilege of being his wife. He was jubilant about the minor effects. The little things, in reality, are the bigger ones that have more impact. He would crack open pistachios and leave a surprise small pile of nuts for me to find and eat.

He would give glances, peeks, stares of adoration and appreciation throughout the day. I knew Alan loved me. He made sure of it. He cheerfully tended all our needs with potable water, laundry, and shopping. Alan cooked breakfast and helped me cook dinner. He helped me into and out of the family truck. He offered his arm for us to walk together because the eye surgery left me unstable. The wild deer in our yard tamed to him without his trying, and the birds flitted in excitement to see him outside as they flew near him, expecting seed to appear for them lavishly to eat.

Remodeling our home, I was cutting costs wherever possible. I was considering having homemade concrete kitchen counters. Alan stunned me with a surprise gift of good–looking granite counters. His sweetness and good nature were never–ending and dearly missed in his absence until we all see him in heaven. Alan had a virtuous heart and was good to me. He was ethical with everyone. He was incapable of any abuse. All physical, emotional, mental, and spiritual levels assumed tremendous respect with tenderly thought–out love and caring. It was a wondrous, corrective cure and appreciated after all I had been through with dysfunctional people and relationships. What a fine Christian man he was.

Alan's smile was gorgeous to behold. He had great big, brown, doe–like eyes. When he smiled, his face was noticeably bright and shining, giving himself to all he gave that smile. He showed sincere delight, acceptance, and appreciation with that radiant smile. When you got his smile, you got all of him lighting up the room. He lit up my world in this beautiful way. His hearty laugh was like none other, and his sense of humor made a person laugh loudly for a long time. I pray I will never forget his endearing little laughs, expressive voice, and quiet, nurturing manner.

The Comforter Holy Spirit played a major role surrounding Alan's being with us no more. Our last days together, blessed with many of God's thoughtful mercies, were good ones. Closure was allowed. Alan tenderly expressed that he was the happiest ever in his life living with me. He had me sing to him O Holy Night because it is one of *my* favorite songs.

I apologized to him again for the swearing (See Chapter 14 "Blessedly Restored Life"). He looked at me, slightly surprised, and earnestly said, "I don't remember you ever swearing." Thank you, my Father! This statement was terrific to me. Alan was curious about this swearing and wanted to know more about it. Our God is extraordinarily remarkable and good! It was miraculous mercy imparted to me to know Alan did not remember and said he never heard the swear words from me.

We earnestly shared all parts of life. He would follow me to watch and hopefully assist with whatever I was up to in our home. We delighted in the Holy Spirit together. Others say it was clear he was adoring and cherishing me in the way he frequently gazed at me. It's with mournful tears I write this chapter.

There was a delicate and picturesque snowstorm the day he died and for a few days afterward. He is not gone. I have the very best of his inward prized gems in who he is inside my heart. It is my vow, with the help of Jesus, to be worthy of being his wife, to be worthy of being his widow.

I nurtured him, tucked him into bed before I got in, and made sure he was comfortable wherever we were.

Our last words together were while holding him in my arms: "My sweet husband, my sweet husband," while he was not feeling so well, as we contentedly embraced in bed. Then, with my arms still wrapped around him, I sat up and loudly and forcefully said,

Snowye: Alan! Do you love God?
Alan: Yes, I love God!
Snowye: Alan! Do you love Jesus?
Alan: Yes, I love Jesus!

Those were our last words together. Alan said he was going downstairs to take a bath to feel better. I asked if he wanted me to go with him, and he said no. It was unusual for us because we shared all things to be near each other.

Indeed, I could not go with him where he was going. I hold gratefulness beyond words for the many mercies of God shown to both of us.

The Comforter Sent by Jesus

I had a premonition of Alan's death. The Comforter came upon me in open vision. Like an intense, momentary electrical shock, I had never felt the Holy Spirit in this way before. It was more like a strong buzz that physically shook me instead of the usual gentle vibrations. I was shown a calendar with a gentle upward moving wisp of white cloud.

Alan will die between your wedding anniversary (19th) and Christmas (25th).
Holy Spirit (to Snowye)

My immediate response was saying you mean Christmas next year, and I'll have that much more time with him. I knew that what the Holy Spirit said was genuine and unavoidable. My tears ran down my cheeks, not knowing what to do. I turned to look at my husband standing behind me. He asked why I was crying, but I couldn't tell him. How come I couldn't tell him? By this time, there was complete shock and denial as well. In my mind, I kept saying to myself, it will be next year, not this year. I have a year to express love and tenderness to him and have him for that long. Complete denial was the case on my part.

Mourning started right away after the open vision. Crying every day for many days, there was an apology to my sweet Alan for what I could not figure out. Typically, he would have been concerned about my crying all day long. Did he know too? I believe he did. He could see the future and has proved it to me many times. Heavenly hearts gave closure for us both in all meaningful ways possible. Closure took place for us in minor occurrences and more significant ways until the day Alan breathed no more. I am rapt by these miraculous gifts that the Holy Spirit gave. I ask why I have all these manifestations (and more) relayed here in *Carillon.* Should only one person benefit in knowing heaven and heavenly beings genuinely exist, all is well with my soul.

We should be happy for our loved ones who have passed on and sleep. Alan sleeps and knows nothing, but in his next moment of consciousness he will experience the exhilaration of resurrection, the glory of New Jerusalem, the new earth, and the rewards of heaven.

I have been at peace. Jesus, the Comforter Holy Spirit, and Angel Daniel restored my truly broken state with comforting love and imparted strength. I harmonized with a unique, euphoric state that resulted in peace and replaced hysterical crying. Alan called the euphoric state from the Comforter, screaming cells.

Also, I am amazingly strengthened with love for the day and the night. It is true Jesus sends the Comforter to those who mourn. Jesus yearns to do so when the Holy Spirit is required to bring tangible well–being and peace when we are distraught beyond reasonable ability. The reassuring solace started with compassion and love that calmed the hysteria and made it so I could sleep. Angel Daniel's strengthening healed more strongly at night, which pulled me through the next day. Despite intense grief, I could make it through the day, knowing soothing by the Holy Spirit and Angel Daniel occurred the moment my head lay on the pillow. Otherwise, I could not have made it with the emotional strain of grief and the resulting physical weakness. I know why so many couples leave this world within days of each other. It's because grief kills.

The first night, there was a bit of opening with crackling in my pineal gland, where the baby's soft spot is at the top of my head. The crackling sound from physical manipulation was the breaking up of hardened mineral deposits (discernment). I could sleep clear through the night until morning. There were still tears all the time, but there was responsible functioning. Our Father is a merciful, majestic, and wonderful God.

Two weeks after Alan's parting, the pineal area had a sensation again while going to sleep. It felt like Angel Daniel was taking his finger, and lightly tracing the spot on top of my head. Suddenly, a jolt of euphoric energy from the Comforter came through the top of my head, flowing to fill my entire body from the inside–out. My cup runneth over. It happened two times with just a few moments in–between. What was this? I know that there has been a change to the innermost part of my being. This change is being examined and pondered.

Possibly completing *Carillon* will show the significance in the future. I have more inspiration to lend comfort and assuagement to all and help them compassionately with their agony, grief, sorrow, and suffering that we all seem to go through.

Alan and I were apart for a year until we united and married. It was the most challenging time ever, being apart and being so much in love. It is like that now. We are apart, but the love held for Alan is tremendous, and I look forward to when we see each together again. It will be a splendid, triumphant, everlasting, blessed life when I see Alan and other loved ones.

The evil one does not win in devastating another human with the strange and wicked ideas of death and grief that the evil one came up with and brought into this world. The evil one made up the idea that we should suffer sorrow at losing loved ones. Humans were not created for these types of episodes that sin brought into our world, making us suffer. We will experience death, but we do not die forever in the end. Gratitude abounds for Jesus Christ in this tremendous victory for humankind that was accomplished on the sacred cross in giving all of us eternal life. I sing praises to Lord Jesus and Father God in gratitude.

Taking the time directly to relax and be open, I was taught a lesson. It became highly personalized in my realization that Jesus died for a sinful human—me. The Holy Spirit gained for me a proper perspective posing the question about whose death was more critical, Jesus' or Alan's? It was a blessed gift, which our Jesus gave in His sacrifice. Without it, Alan's death would be eternal, with no chance of me ever laughing with Alan again.

This insight, through God's grace and mercy, brought about my extreme gratitude to Lord Jesus for providing eternal Life by sacrifice on His divine cross. Through God's mercy and grace, it had given me the gift of gratitude. Gratitude imparted a state which allowed inward peace. Together, gratitude and peace granted me an environment where I could Love. In this way, a state of terrible pain and agonizing grief gave way to the beautiful feeling of Love.

Holy Spirit's tender words and ministry of uplifting and euphoric physical vibrations, along with the love and strengthening conveyed by Angel Daniel, kept me in tranquil peacefulness wherein love lived inside me to be expressed.

It was an extreme mercy of our Father and Jesus to put love in the place of searing grief. People around me would remark that I was glowing.

There were small messages from the Comforter Holy Spirit and other heavenly hearts. To know they care for us ultimately is an incredible mystery. My wish is for all to understand and grasp the Truth. The Godhead Trinity is tangible. The Trinity can and will minister—and be perceptibly present in our daily lives.

Holy Spirit's part about "financial quarterly" was perplexing. Holy Spirit and Angel Daniel gave help and guidance on what tasks needed to be accomplished and in what order for financial matters after Alan's passing. I appreciated this because I was in a complete mess of an inability to think about anything. Sure enough, the funeral home told me that some insurance companies sometimes do not pay the benefit for three–four months to get the profit of quarterly interest money first, before distributing any financial outlay. Angel Daniel alerted me to state taxes that needed to be accomplished, having dealt with only federal taxes in the past. The nudge with information was right on time because I completed the tax papers that night, and they were due to be filed the next day. The following are words of the Comforter to another bereaved person, which helped me.

> Your daughter is no longer in the past—she is now in your future.
> From: "A Powerful Word For Those Who Have Lost Loved Ones"
> by Michael Bradley
> https://www.bible-knowledge.com/lost-loved-ones/
> (Accessed: December 28, 2017)

Mourning and sorrow are heartfelt, but situations are much worse for many others. I enjoy a roof over my head and a clean, dry bed. I can prepare food to have physical strength. Bible studies enrich the day. How many have a cold street for a bed with no one to comfort them with a touch or show we care about them in their misery? How many are starving in this world? My cares, in comparison, are nothing. Especially when Jesus showed three empty places amidst a portrayal of shadows, saying it was where Alan and I (plus another—I know now to be Zach) would be standing. I realized, too, that our souls' salvation are not guaranteed, presumed, or assumed without incurring a risk we won't be saved. I continually work toward a Christ–like character; to exhibit the Fruit of the Spirit. This is an important task to be pleasant in God's eyes.

There are many sorrowful tears. Would I want this bitter cup to pass from me? No. First, it is God's will. Second, not grieving and minimizing Alan's depth in what he means to me is not an honorable option. Alan means enough for me to take the bitter cup.

It is Jesus' way too with tears—although the Comforter and Angel Daniel provide alleviation. Tears are necessary for a person's mental/emotional health in the grieving process. Jesus allows the emotional outpouring of tears in His tender caring for our complete selves' well–being. Nothing in His great love and concern for every human being is halfway with our holy Lord and Guardian.

> If you love him, you should be happy for him.
> Holy Spirit (to Snowye)

> [26]But the Comforter, which is the Holy Ghost, whom the Father will send in my name, he shall teach you all things, and bring all things to your remembrance, whatsoever I have said unto you.
> (John 14:26)

> No extremes.
> Not as thou will, but as our Father wilt.
> Financial quarterly.
> Holy Spirit (to Snowye)

> You need to start learning state taxes.
> Angel Daniel (to Snowye)

Special Chortle

There was no secret side to Alan. There was no ulterior agenda. He would come into the room just stand there—staring at and enjoying—what he saw in his wife, church family, and surroundings.

I prayed not to fail recalling his small warm chuckle that is difficult to describe. In the last days before his death, Alan was laughing this way, more often, in complete joy and contentment that was so charming. After his passing, I did not eat for a long time. Our friend took me out and made sure I ate a small meal.

Getting up from the table, I laughed the same chortle as Alan! Jesus blessedly gave me the adorable laugh so that now I will never forget it. I had never laughed like that before. I could not see Alan's face when he made that sweet laugh. O, my lovable Alan was endearing! The abundant mercies of our Father, Jesus, and Holy Spirit abound and are incomparable. Despite an enveloping loss, they gave me meaning to life, giving my soul the bread of life. Because of our Lord and Savior Christ Jesus—Alan is not in my past; he is in my future.

13

Bell Chimes

The previous "Chapter 12" explains some of the many reasons there were no regrets with the experience of knowing Alan. Lack of regret is another tender mercy given by God, The Monarch of the Universe. We lived all the valuable moments as they should have been. In our Father's incredible mercy, the Holy Spirit gave me a premonition, difficult to accept, foretelling of Alan's soon passing. I am sure the Holy Spirit gave Alan this insight as well. There was closure for both of us in the things said and done. Those intimate exchanges were a blessing in assisting the mourning process.

It is essential to live life with developed Christian values, beginning with obeying our Father's law outlined in the Ten Commandments, which reveals our Father's desirable character. The most we can do is repent of our sins and accept Jesus' gift of forgiveness and salvation. The veil is high, and the evil is dense clear up to that veil.

Our perceptions of what might be good are skewed and possibly unrealistic. The only hope of being worthy to live in heaven is surrendering our entire life into Jesus' proficient and skillful hands.

Alan and I let Jesus be in charge of our lives through prayer and asking for Him to be our core. This accomplished, at least in a small way, having intense motivation to do His will, not ours. To accomplish Jesus' and God's will was foremost in Alan's and my daily determinations and this brought about the life we wanted full of goodness and purpose.

We had seven short years of married life together. Thank You, Almighty Father, eternally and gratefully for giving Alan to me. I look forward to knowing Alan, where there is no more misery, remorse, or tears. Instead, there is joy, honor, appreciation, completeness, purpose, respect, and devotion for everyone, forever and ever. The real blessing is that evil will never return.

After our extended courtship, Alan asked me to marry, and he drove by the chapel daily to show and remind me. When I happily said yes, I thought of when, what dress, where, who to invite, what reception, etc. Instead, Alan grabbed my hand harder and more firmly than usual. He led me to the car right then. We got into the car, and right away, Alan grabbed my hand the same way and would not let go. I asked why he held my hand so firmly and did not let go.

Alan: I will never let you go.

I didn't know he was taking me to the chapel. In this tender way, he was honoring Jesus in our getting married right then, that very moment, because he knew about my vision with Jesus well, along with what Jesus said to me (See Chapter 5 "Footpath Like None Other") on the narrow footpath.

He held my hand, getting out of the car and going into the chapel to be married. His grasp was unwavering, and he wouldn't let go. When we approached the chapel, I said if there were cigarette burns on the furniture when we went in, I would not get married in this place. He said there were no cigarette burns, and it was charming inside. He was correct, and it was tasteful and appealing. The justice of the peace had arranged for a special Christian ceremony to be performed instead of the civil one. We were happily married in The Chapel of the Bells. I will sing Alan's praises. I will sing the Father's songs of praise. *Carillon* contains these sweet and heartfelt songs.

Alan contentedly wound our grandfather clock every week, just before the Sabbath. The bells' harmonious chimes in the clock pass the time until that Great Day when we see our Blessed Redeemer Jesus descending in the clouds with Angels, displaying His incredible glory. The guidance of our Father, Jesus and the Comforter, along with incredibly loving angels, provides the needed meaning and fulfillment in my life until that Great Day of Jesus' second coming when none of this material earthly world's trials and woes matter anymore.

This is especially true with the mesmerizing and soft snow falling silently and serenely. Like the white, hushed, and peaceful snowy day my dear, sweet Alan went to sleep.

Do I Love God? Yes, I Love God!
Do I Love Jesus? Yes, I Love Jesus!

Mercy, Grace, Gratitude, Peace ~ the ability to love

Alan rests in an old country cemetery surrounded by a vast pine forest on a steep hill overlooking splendid mountain views. It's a wild setting. Deer roam among the ancient graves of the original settlers of the area. Zach knew Alan, and he likes to visit Alan's resting place with me to say prayers and place flowers.

[10]In whose hand is the soul of every living thing, and the breath of all mankind.
(Job 12:10)

A Better
Life

Blessedly Restored Life

Growing up as the second eldest and eldest girl in a family of seven children was challenging because they expected a lot from me. The other children watched me for a role model for which I wasn't suited. Lacking maturity and being a child myself didn't produce a role model reflecting the idealistic expectations of the younger ones and others. We were four girls and three boys. My parents saw we were well cared for, and I thank the Father our parents could afford all of us with no financial strife. There was the advantage of a traditional family with my parents being married until they both passed away. They loved each other immensely, along with all of us children who were theirs.

Parents and relatives never mentioned Judaism in our home, but our mother revealed that my father's parents and grandparents were Jewish. They had dropped their Jewish religion for a reason that no one knew. A large picture of Jesus was in my grandmother's bedroom. My grandparents' home was Jewish, and great–grandpa wore his yarmulke inside the house and out. My grandmother was born in my great–grandparent's home, and it was the same home where my grandmother gave birth to my father.

Judaism and its teachings weren't a part of our spiritual pursuits while living at home and growing up. Our rearing was without religion. My parents thought we should all determine individual spiritual paths. They encouraged us to attend any church we chose. During my teenage years, the evil one had already begun its influence where it wasn't considered cool to take part in church or have Christian religious beliefs. Saint Patrick's Day was about being pinched either way, for wearing, or not wearing, orange or green. I didn't appreciate it one bit, and it didn't seem to be religious–like behavior to me. My views on Christianity weren't positive. My thinking was, why would I need a priest or Jesus when I spoke to God directly?

My father's activities in spiritual journeys led to his interest in metaphysical pursuits. He was an honorary thirty–third degree mason. His mother was a member of the order of the eastern star, resulting in introductions to new age paths like ECKANKAR, Scientology and Rosicrucian teachings. The institutions we investigated were not witches–type religions like Wicca. Black magic, the occult, spells, and negativity were fortunately not a part of my growing up. The organizations looked into disapproved of Satanism, witchcraft, and black magic rites. We considered the Ouija Board a satanic activity not to play or suffer the evil consequences. The metaphysical beliefs considered that praying was making harmful spells aimed at others and infringing on a person's free will. I found this proven untrue because it was with prayers being said for healing that I received miraculous cures that I am extremely grateful for. Metaphysical pursuits hold no belief in the existence of Satan. This is Satan's greatest accomplishment in people believing he doesn't exist. The intention with metaphysics is to become a co–worker with God. I don't believe these things. Satan enticed Eve with the same ideas. Eve was charmed into becoming as a god to get her to eat the forbidden fruit from the tree of knowledge. Eve's sin committed by her was in not obeying God.

I dropped the various metaphysical religious paths in my early twenty's. I believed in God but had no spiritual pursuits after this until I started looking into Christian churches to join, intending to fight the evil in our world.

Bible studies swayed Alan and me to select a Sabbatarian doctrine. We were baptized by complete immersion together in the waters of a flowing river in the beautiful mountains with pine trees. We began the dignified observance of the seventh–day Sabbath on Saturday, rejecting a first–day Sabbath on Sunday, declared by man.

There is now fellowship and Bible study in our home. Praise is to God; life is enjoyable in the fullness that simplicity provides in devout gatherings. Truth is simple and stable; sin is complicated and volatile.

Slowly, step–by–step, God has had His hand in my life. This has been to prepare for a life with our Lord and Champion Jesus. Lord Jesus, being in my life has brought intimacy on an elegant and contentment–filled level. There is a purpose in my life. The world now makes sense in knowing about the controversy being played out between good and evil. Biblical conceptions through Prophet Ellen G. White bring heartfelt peace and security. I spend time in repentance, studying the Scripture (which is wished started forty years ago), preparing this book, and preparing to spread the Three Angels' Messages. Heavenly communications and improvements in my character are hopefully continuing to take place.

I keep a journal of communications and occurrences with heavenly hearts. The journal is essential to connect with those who pursue our best interests in ways we cannot fathom. It is not always easy. I appreciate all the good and the atrocious trials gone through. The trick would be to be thankful while actually going through a difficulty, suffering, or hardship.

> The test is in the moment.
> Zach

> Eternity is only a breath away.
> Zach

With Zach's insightful mindset, one is fully open to the lesson being taught to us by our divine Father. Both good and the opposite catalysts have molded me into who I am today. The lesson given to me in surrender to Lord Jesus is an example of what learning Christian biblical principles has provided in desirable character development. Hopefully, spiritual growth with its healthy expansion takes an inward hold with studying the Bible. I will always strive to comprehend more about Christianity's sacred and mysterious truths.

Surrender to Lord Jesus

I had no clue what surrendering to Jesus was besides relaxing and saying so. Parts of being reared in my childhood home demanded no swearing or swear words. Twice, I saw my brothers getting their mouths washed out with soap, which took care of any likelihood for me to curse. After the soap incentives, no one in our home dared to speak insolent obscenities. So uttering profanity had never been a part of my behavior, even as an adult.

Out of the blue, anger and swearing like a sailor began with me. Fortunately, it was only at home—my poor husband (Alan). I continually prayed about it, saying this was not me. I was desperate with a constant litany, pleading and asking, where did this come from? What is this anger—even blaming some nearby demon for doing it? This is not me! All my life, obscenities were never a part. Morning and night, I prayed about it, asking Jesus to please have it stop. Please, dear Jesus, have whatever is causing this foul language to please cease, disintegrate and go away! A couple of days might pass with entreaties answered, providing peace and patience like before. However, the cursing would still happen over and over.

It was embarrassing to ask forgiveness from my husband—so many times. Not the asking, but the number of failures and times asking forgiveness was exasperating. How could my husband know this was not some depraved character trait that had been a part of me that was just now coming out after so many years of marriage, as if I had hidden it from him? My honor was at stake. Standing in the kitchen during eclipse day as I was preparing breakfast, I asked my Lord and Savior Jesus to please take the swearing affliction from me. I didn't know what my prayer would bring, nor that was it actually surrendering.

My Lord and God Jesus, who I love, it seems it is to go on forever, this awful swearing. I can only acknowledge that it must be me after all this time. It is who I am. I cannot say any longer that this is not me. It has been too long since this behavior. Dearest Jesus, who I love, I am so sorry for what you get in filthy rags, lack of righteousness, and a sorry lot, am I. I can no longer do anything to help myself stop the outbursts of terrible words that are degrading. But here I am for you to do with, as you wish. What I try in this matter is all given up, and I am in Your loving hands to do with as You wish in all things. Please forgive me for the fallen and unworthy person who I am. Please use me for some good, if it can be at all possible despite my foul words. A swearing person is not a good representative of your Word. Especially after what You lovingly did for me when You came and got me. Please forgive me and stay with me, Jesus. For You are my light, and without You there is only darkness. Amen.

Instantly, after my prayer ended, the Holy Spirit increased in vibrations and joy. The love was graceful, peaceful, and pleasantly surrounding. In the open vision, Jesus reached out and took me into His full embrace. Jesus was holding me closely with my side against His chest, in His zealous arms, as I had my arms crossed and lowered in front of me, head bowed in humility. It was a comforting security with calmness and a beautiful illustration that I did not want to end. Being held with His arms holding me, He spoke in His vibrant, devoted, kind, smooth and deep voice,

Lord Jesus: You are surrendered.

His spoken words were noticeably and mysteriously a command and a statement simultaneously. I could feel the coarser, loosely woven fabric of His white robe, which was like a lighter summer weight. I could feel His strength and the divine beauty of His endless love emanating from Him and touching the inner parts of my soul.

Then the vision shifted. Jesus asked permission to place a tube on me as He showed it to me. To say no to my Lord would never be an option. I was inside an opaque, broad, smooth tube that spread, so my hands touched the sides, and the tube stretched upward over my head five feet. The only light that allowed me to see came from the round opening above. No amount of turning or twisting inside the tube, pushing against the sides of the tube, jumping up to hold the top of the rim, or trying to grasp the smooth sides with my hands worked. There was no way out of the tube. Jesus reached from the top of the tube, took my hand, and effortlessly pulled me out.

From being inside the tube with no way out, I realized that this was how it was with the swearing that burdened me. I gained compassion for others dealing with addictions, afflictions, and serious situations. I used to believe people lacked self–discipline to overcome cravings, destructive mindsets, abusive and sinful lifestyles. It's the undoubted truth that Lord Jesus is the only way out of these disorders. Being surrendered and inside the tube gave me more complete and understanding compassion. I was harmonizing with others who find themselves helpless with no escape from Satan's diseases and misery–driven behaviors that destroy themselves and those around them.

I gratefully now hold kindheartedness for those ravaged by Satan when these people wish for, deserve, and are destined by our Creator to prosper and have goodness in their lives.

I learned it isn't a lack of self-discipline or particular circumstances that allow hardship and torment to continue. Jesus is in charge, and only He can do all things—if allowed. We lack control over our own lives. Goodness and all we deserve in a good life result from allowing Jesus to be in charge of everything. Zach's jubilant marriage proposal included that we keep Lord Jesus as our divine centerpiece.

Three years later, I was still asking how compassion relates to surrender. I discerned that compassion is the key to surrender. Surrender comes from having a compassionate heart for Jesus Christ's consecrated toil on the cross. To have vivid mercy and an in-depth affinity for what took place on the cross cannot help but result in surrender to our impeccable Deliverer. The opposite occurs in allowing the evil one's dread command in a damaging, sinful lifestyle. Our magnificent and paramount Father loans our breath to us. The state of surrender to Lord Jesus is accomplished moment-to-moment. Surrender only completes itself through Jesus. Discernment showed that the only way out is through our Lord Jesus. He accomplishes His fervent will for us in our lives through our complete surrender and our devoted, willing obedience to Him.

Pray for Jesus to surrender us. To pray for strength to surrender is an appeal to accomplish it. We cannot accomplish it ourselves. Only Jesus can surrender us, if we allow Him.

End Times Array

15

Three Angels' Messages

Understanding we are in the era and end times of the three angels' messages is according to what we prove in the Bible's writings of prophecy. The three angels' announcement is a warning to stay away from the deceptions rampant in the world and to come back to honor and worship our Creator. We should also keep His Commandments and have the Faith of Savior Jesus. It is a crucial message to the universe. Decisions are being made (right now) about where we spend eternity—be it in heaven—or destroyed into nothingness by burning fire into ashes with no life or existence forever.

We recognize and worship God as our Creator, especially just before the time of Lord of Lords Jesus' second coming, because it is our last opportunity. We want the proper fullness of joyous life given to us by spending eternity with God and our precious Lord Jesus.

The Three Angels' Messages are a sounding, a warning, and a cry for this last chance to enjoy eternity in heaven. It is now or never that we get right with our Creator to live and have life everlasting rather than eternal nothingness. Our Father will destroy the wicked by fire in the end. However, in God's loving mercy, they don't burn forever, as depicted in common scenarios of hell. According to the Bible, the fire and smoke go out, and there is no more existence for the wicked.

> The harvest of life is character, and it is this that determines destiny, both for this life and for the life to come.
> White, Ellen G.
> *Education*, p. 110

Keeping the Faith of Jesus

Faith *in* Jesus is not the same as the faith *of* Jesus. We want to develop and hold in ourselves the faith *of* Jesus. The faith of Jesus is the faith that the Son possessed in His Father. Lord Jesus' agonizing prayer while sweating blood in the Garden of Gethsemane shows this extraordinary faith He had in our Father.

> [39]And he went a little farther, and fell on his face, and prayed, saying, O my Father, if it be possible, let this cup pass from me: nevertheless not as I will, but as thou wilt.
> (Matthew 26:39)

Jesus perspired blood and asked to remove the bitter cup from Him should there be any other way. But Jesus had so much faith in our majestic and powerful God that He trusted He would rise again and He would save Adam's fallen race.

Mark of the Beast

The decision to receive the beast's mark is by bended knee and obedience given to the evil one. This would be with our thoughts (in the forehead) or with our actions (in the hand), or both, as described in Revelation 14:9–12.

One sure way we gain the mark of the beast is by keeping the first day—Sunday—as the day of worshipping our God. Sunday worship disobeys the fourth commandment given by God. Soon, Sunday laws will try to force all people to worship on this human–made Sabbath. The evil one wants to be worshiped in God's place and hates everything to do with God.

They will blame those not worshipping on Sunday for the evil occurrences happening in the world, like earthquakes, floods, famine, disease/pestilences and other disasters that take human life. Government representatives will pass a death decree involved with this union of Church and State to kill anyone not keeping Sunday worship.

It is the evil one's dream come true. Anything meaningful to God—His law—His creation of humankind, and earth, Satan relentlessly targets for destruction through any means possible.

> [15]And he had power to give life unto the image of the beast, that the image of the beast should both speak, and cause that as many as would not worship the image of the beast should be killed.
> (Revelation 13:15)

[9]And the third angel followed them, saying with a loud voice, If any man worship the beast and his image, and receive his mark in his forehead, or in his hand, [10]The same shall drink of the wine of the wrath of God, which is poured out without mixture into the cup of his indignation; and he shall be tormented with fire and brimstone in the presence of the holy angels, and in the presence of the Lamb: [11]And the smoke of their torment ascendeth up for ever and ever: and they have no rest day nor night, who worship the beast and his image, and whosoever receiveth the mark of his name. [12]Here is the patience of the saints: here are they that keep the commandments of God, and the faith of Jesus.
(Revelation 14:9–12)

I saw the leading men of the earth consulting together, and Satan and his angels busy around them. I saw a writing, copies of which were scattered in different parts of the land, giving orders that unless the saints should yield their peculiar faith, give up the Sabbath, and observe the first day of the week, the people were at liberty after a certain time to put them to death.
White, Ellen G.
Early Writings, pp. 282, 283.

16

Writer's Essence

This chapter is more in an assortment that portrays the writer's outlooks. My viewpoints have changed for the better (by far) from being with Lord Jesus that Sabbath day, January 30, 2010, in a glorious open vision.

I believe it is not okay to act on, nor feel another person needs to be made inferior or made into failure to get ahead. Consider there is room at the top for everyone instead. Reach out a hand and help others up to the top. Make successes of all those near you, rather than have disappointment and decay littered about your unclean feet. People trusting you with their lives results from recognizing a good and honorable character. Two letters of recognition for my résumé state they trust me with their life. I did not solicit those statements from two different people who don't know each other. These are the relationships worthy of a person's time and diligent effort.

Dream it first, then we can achieve it. The accomplishment of dreams usually entails enthusiastic and focused work.

There is no love without respect. Respect all people, if nothing else, as fellow creations of our Father who loves us all. What other attitude would we hold toward Father's fellow designs that He loves so much?

Blessed Love

What is love? Kind acts with holding a kind heart should be the base from which we operate.

> Responsibility without love makes
> us inconsiderate.
> Power without love makes us cruel.
> Belief without love makes us fanatics.
> Intelligence without love makes us dishonest.
> Lao Tzu (604 BC–531 BC)

> Love is the wish to bestow the fullness of
> joyous life on someone.
> Snowye's biological Father
> Source unknown.

> Love isn't what most people say it is. Love
> is much more important than a feeling; it's
> an intense commitment.
> Zach (Snowye's husband)

To think and speak poorly about another has an unacceptable, adverse effect and consequence on them. Life is tough enough for everyone. Why add to it? We do not need the ruination and judgments about character or actions to add more sorrow while living in and dealing with this world—the evil one's command for now. Murmuring is terribly devastating.

Also, do not believe people do not know how you feel about them. They do. Please use self–discipline, worship, and our Lord Jesus to harbor zero ill thoughts and damaging feelings toward others. Separate God's fellow creation from their actions. Love God's fellow creation. Forgive their actions.

Men are wonderful. I am not a man basher. Men have a tremendous responsibility in making sure there is a home and those living there are happy. To keep their wife happy, they wind up agreeing and giving in. They accuse men in this day and age if they put their foot down with the arrogant woman (expecting his services for her happiness in a harlot–type of relationship). Men are worth respecting. They love and many times seem to have the deepest feelings.

The man protects the lives of those dear to him, along with humankind itself, possibly giving his own life. A man giving up his own life for others' survival is a part of a man's nobility. Any decent person would respect and honor that nobility at all times. Women are the same; however, the nobleness of heart seems to be overlooked too much for our noble–hearted men.

Forgiveness is liberation for the person forgiving rather than the perpetrator. Holding non–forgiveness in our hearts is a destructive burden. Non–forgiveness will cause a downward spiral of negativity, taking one away from our Lord Jesus and the heavenly beings. It will harden a heart. A hardened heart is closed to our Creator, Lord Jesus, Holy Spirit, and the Angels' presence in our lives.

We all know what correct behavior is, naturally. The way to develop honor, inner security, and the best fruits possible is to do what is right. Always do the right thing. What else do we possess but our good word and, hopefully, our good name? It is only our excellent character we take to heaven. Should it be the opposite of the right outcome chosen in our actions, at least we tried? We all err. Vow to yourself and God to not err in the same way again. This is part of an apology too. It is the most and best we can do. An apology should be specific in details about the error committed. The particular components allow the other person to forgive the offender. How can anyone forgive something they don't know what to disregard? It's not okay to ask forgiveness from someone with just a general statement like, "Please forgive me for whatever I have wronged you." This type of statement is deceitful, and you won't gain forgiveness because it's human nature to resent that deceit.

A peaceful state of mind that is simple and cleared, holding love for God, Jesus, and the comforter Holy Spirit provides the needed environment (within ourselves) for heavenly hearts to be present and ultimately produce countless good works for us in our best interests. Physically, for me, Holy Spirit manifests in a joyous vibration of all cells in my body.

Life is about here and now. The past is gone, and the future lacks existence. Reality is only here and in the present moment. Therefore, what we can manage, change, and live in—is only right now. Apply this alertness to the moment. The moments, not the years, make up our lives and who we are. We should only strive for the very best, nothing less. This is the basis for genuinely learning and gaining from life's lessons. Be the best you can be, moment–by–moment. I go all out to be the best I can be for when Jesus returns.

It is wasting time being anything but who you are—absolute freedom rests in being ourselves. There is freedom in the moment with Jesus in our lives. Being in the moment is key in surrendering to and living with Jesus at the helm of our existence. Gain to the good in many and mighty blessings affecting our real lives can be had in this. Jesus, being our centerpiece, means everything goes according to His plan, and it benefits us and those around us in all areas of life and its turmoil. This brings success to our lives. It's the crucial difference I have noticed since my open vision with Jesus Christ. I now hold successes and positive outcomes instead of Satan–influenced failures resulting from my reasonable and good efforts.

Many seek being loved. The blessings of love are in the giving of it versus receiving it, because one feels love when they are flowing and giving it. Allow others to experience love by allowing their loving of you. A loving person attracts other loving persons, bringing peace and prosperity. A person is a grown–up and an adult when they achieve knowing themselves. One should know who and what they are with Jesus being in charge and the Bible's scriptural teachings. Until then, we only see ourselves when we look at others. When one knows who they are, they can discern themselves as separate from what they perceive in another person. We can comprehend other people's characters as well. An adult can only hope to come close to relaying, connecting, and conveying thoughts to another self–aware adult.

The Bible instructs and shows us all the fine details and potential scenarios for what it is to develop a noble character.

Essentially, the fruit of the spirit displays a noble character. Following the Ten Commandments is just the beginning of refinement toward possessing a noble stature. The Bible portrays life situations that expand on the Ten Commandments. Life situations described in the Bible give us an understanding of the desired character we should seek and examples of the opposite, which brings eternal death.

> The race is not to the swift, but to those
> who wait upon the LORD.
> Zach
> (Inspired by Ecclesiastes 9:11)

A relationship is most fulfilling on all levels, with Jesus as the focus. Look in the mirror. Be unconditionally and thoroughly frank. Keep what you approve of in yourself. Work and sincerely improve what we perceive to be lacking. Begin with accomplishing and pursuing the Ten Commandments respectably to live by and honorably obey in everything you do. Read the word of God daily. The correct version of the Bible—the King James Version—is the word of our Holy God. The evil one has produced other bibles with changes that seem fine on the surface; but in reality, make the Trinity's redemption plan slanted and unrecognizable.

Optimism with contentment is a choice. At the worst of times, we can realize that there are others much worse off than ourselves. Realizing that women in Africa are attacked and their arm cut off above the elbow when collecting firewood gives pause to how well we live. Firewood collecting is necessary to cook meals to feed their families. Women in Africa need their arm to hold and nurse their baby. How can anyone devastated by their circumstances compare absolute horror to such as these and not hearten with encouragement? At the very least, a realistic perspective of our sufferings can be determined. Communion with Jesus and knowing Him are necessary for our lives, bringing vitality. What does a parent wish most for their child? Most parents' aspiration is for their child's happiness despite what challenges life brings. Be optimistic and grateful. Be that positive–minded, cheerful Abraham's Child of God—for Him.

Positivity is a choice. It is also a healthful state to be positive. Look at the good for any situation. It is a desirable habit and training of the mind to develop. It doesn't mean ignoring the prevalent negativity in our world. We need to be attentive to negativity, guard against it, and address it. The problem is that so many are primarily negative, operating from this viewpoint. The educational system teaches to have a negative outlook and a destructive mindset, resulting in failures. Often, this is required to be accepted by a potential friend. You're okay and make a friend if you moan and groan about people in your life. Dare to be different.

Our Creator's way is a positive outlook. Pay close consideration to the thoughts. Catch the views and change the thoughts to be positive. It is a discipline and conscious effort when first attempting this. After some repetition, it becomes second nature and more easily accomplished.

In seeking to change your diet, start in the grocery store. We will not eat it if it is not in the kitchen. A vegan diet seems to be best in these end times. Meat, dairy, and fat of the past were not concentrated reservoirs of poisons that the evil one goes out of its way for us to ingest. There are many things we can simply do without in order to be the best we can be.

Take the time to thank individual cells in the body for the enthusiastic and dedicated work allowing existence in this earth world. Take the time also to issue love to each cell in the body. Recognize and appreciate the intricate, miraculous, God–given bodily systems. Thank our magnificent God for His brilliance.

Murmuring

It's a trick of the devil. I thought murmuring was simple, innocent, and of no consequence. Just a brief whisper or something muttered under the breath that wasn't worth repeating or hearing, anyway. No big deal, so what? It's mentioned nineteen times in the Holy Bible. Aaron and his sister Miriam were both severely chastised by God for murmuring. Miriam contracted leprosy. I wondered what was so bad about murmuring that our Father God would harshly punish someone.

So I looked up the word murmur and its synonyms. It is absolutely a horrible abomination to murmur. Rather than murmuring, it would be best to focus on the reverse. We can create a rich charisma with murmur's antonyms as a part of who we are: Calm, peace, serenity, cessation, quietude, repose, composure, patience, compliment, praise, harmony, happiness, acceptance, approval, contentedness, sanction, applause, health. Looking into murmuring was important. Those who indulge in murmuring should develop the fruit of the spirit instead. I work with training myself to think differently and be aware not to gossip or portray bad things about other people. God loves us all and wants unique intimacy with every person. Their experiences are their own for growing a noble character, provided by our Father. Everyone needs our support and tender kindness.

> To err is human, to forgive, divine.
> English Poet Alexander Pope
> *An Essay on Criticism,*
> *Part II*, 1711

> As we near the end of time, falsehood will be so mingled with truth, only those guided by the Holy Spirit will distinguish truth from error.
> White, Ellen G.
> SDA Bible Commentary,
> vol.7, p. 907.1

> It is the work of Satan to seek some stain upon the character of Christ's followers, to talk of their faults, and magnify their errors.
> White, Ellen G.
> *Review and Herald.*
> November 6, 1883.

How Come?

One thing I want to understand is—why? How come there are all these sojourns with heavenly beings when I found out that it is a scarce occurrence for most people? One answer is, "Wow, I sure must have needed a lot of help!" I was so far gone that our Savior Jesus was required to extend to me His personal intervention!

Maybe the visits are because I can handle it without too much upsetting my mental/emotional state. My professional profiling places me as intuitive, first and thinker, second.

Although, I must admit, with my dear husband's death—how it all fits in, handling it all and coping, keeping purposeful meaning, and putting it all into perspective—is more complex than it might usually be. Simultaneously, God, the Comforter, Angel Daniel, and Lord Jesus make it possible with their tender ministry, grace, and mercies. I can only accept an unknown reason our heavenly Father established a relationship and provided medical alleviations for my well–being in the ways He has. He knows everything in advance from the end to the beginning. I'm joyous because I can be confident of our Father's victory in the good versus evil crisis now playing out as the universes watch. And that we can believe the truths in the Bible that are given to us for help and guidance. The Trinity is something that everyone can realize.

It would be rewarding if others heard and encountered heavenly beings, too. Joyousness would come from sharing experiences and learning from them. Knowing that divine hearts are genuine gives security and purpose in my life. They care, see, keep track of us, and hear us. Assuredly know: We are never alone. I remember those video cards kept in a box.

> I sought the LORD, and he heard
> me, and delivered me from
> all my fears
> (Psalms 34:4)

I have ongoing contemplations about an explanation for the extraordinary occurrences with the Godhead Trinity and the holy angels. What is crucial for me is that people would hopefully realize that heavenly beings and heaven are absolutely in existence and authentic. It is for our benefit and guidance to be our very best. It is the same for everyone. Our Lord Jesus is in all of our lives. Do people know this? Do they want to be aware of His presence? Could they handle the change for good and success in their lives?

> Be not forgetful to entertain strangers:
> for thereby some have entertained
> angels unawares.
> (Hebrews 13:2)

Should we want to contact heavenly hearts, the best encouragement I can give would be to create within ourselves an environment wherein the divine beings from heaven can function in our personal lives. This would be a firm grounding in considering and obeying the Ten Commandments amid all our moments, thoughts, and actions during our waking hours. It would take some effort and thought, and it would, without a doubt, allow the opportunity while dealing with others to act differently. Do not lie. Lying to make it easier for another person, no matter the situation, is not okay. This includes withholding or tweaking information if asked. White lies are not white; they are as dark as evil. The habit of lying prevents maturing as a human to hold grace, dignity, and wisdom.

I also encourage to actively and purposely develop for a moral character the fruit of the Spirit: Love, Joy, Peace, Long-suffering (patience), Gentleness, Goodness, Faith, Meekness and Temperance. Ask for the Holy Spirit's baptism in wisdom, knowledge, understanding, discernment, strength through grace, and recognition of our need for these things. I pray to be pleasing before God's eyes. O yes—those sparkling, indescribable eyes are full of intimacy, kindness, understanding, powerful and relaxed gentleness!

It's because of Satan. We seem to live two lives, our inner and our outer. I believe many more would reveal their inner experiences except for this environment in our world designed by the devil to nullify the heavenly beings. If we reveal experiences with God, Lord Jesus, and angels, we are labeled as: Crazy, liars, and fundamentalist frauds looking for attention and self–glorification. If only they knew heavenly hearts are factual and closer to us than we think. Believe in the presence of holy manifestations. Talk to them. I spoke in prayer, and Lord Jesus accommodated beyond expression with my met needs, fulfillment in life's purposes, and much more in making my life whole.

I didn't know I could love so much. My genuinely loving God and loving Jesus imparts strength to me. Holy Spirit, Angel Daniel, and the heavenly host make up my moments, my life.

Thank you, Our Lord of Angels, Jesus—for Life.

God Detests A Liar

16 These six things doth the LORD hate: yea seven are an abomination unto him:

17 A proud look, a lying tongue, and hands that shed innocent blood.

(Proverbs 6:16, 17)

22 Lying lips are abomination to the LORD: but they that deal truly are his delight.

(Proverbs 12:22)

But the fruit of the Spirit is

love
joy
peace
longsuffering
gentleness
goodness
faith
meekness
temperance

against such there is no law
(Galatians 5:22-23)

Some of
Our LORD's Titles

Son of God	Prince of Peace
Creator	Lord of Angels
Great High Priest	Son of David
Christ the LORD	The True Vine
Commander of Heaven	Prince of Life
Minister of the Sanctuary	The Good Shepherd
Savior of the Adamic Race	Resurrection and the Life
Prince of Kings	Christ Our Mediator
He Whom Angels Worship	Alpha and Omega
Sun of Righteousness	Christ Our Passover
Prince of Heaven	Light of the World
King of Kings	The Way and the Truth
Just One	Messiah the Prince
The Drink of Heaven	The Light and the Life
Anointed One	Son of Man
Bright and Morning Star	Captain of Salvation
Lord of Heaven and Earth	Lily of the Valley
Lord of Glory	The Messiah
True Educator	Advocate Christ
The Bread of Heaven	Lord of Lords
Majesty of Heaven	Lamb of God

Definition of *Carillon*

carillon
In American English

kærə ˌlɑn / us occas., kəˈrɪljən
noun

1. | ...
7. | a set of stationary bells, each producing a different musical tone, now usually sounded by means of a keyboard
8. | a musical instrument that produces such tones electronically
9. | a composition for the carillon
10. | an organ stop producing a carillonlike [sic] sound

From: *Collins Definition of Carillon.*
https://www.collinsdictionary.com/us/dictionary/english/carillon
(Accessed November 1, 2020)

Author's Note: They pronounce Carillon differently in America than in England. Please see the website above to hear both ways. Carillon is a word for a melody or song played on a set of bells. It is also the material tower of bells itself.

Daniel

Daniel is from the Hebrew name: לִאֱיֵנֶד
(*Daniyyel*) meaning "God is my judge"

From "Behind the Name"
https://www.behindthename.com/names/usage/biblical
(Accessed September 3, 2017)

Scriptural Index

Old Testament

Numbers
24:16---------106

II Kings
19:35---------100

Job
12:10---------160

Psalms
17:8,9---------27
33:6-----------67
34:4-----------186
37:5-----------52
51:10----------62
51:11----------80
77:18,19-------73
95:6-----------62
119:8----------62
119:10---------62
147:4----------67

Proverbs
6:16,17-------189
12:22---------189
30:5----------114

Ecclesiastes
12:13----------62

Isaiah
1:18----------113
43:1-----------80
65:24---------114

Jeremiah
32:27---------111
33:3-----------51

Ezekiel
1:10----------132
1:15----------130
1:17----------132
10:12---------132

Malachi
3:10----------114
3:15-17-------144

New Testament

Matthew
9:35----------114
21:22---------114
26:39---------174

Luke
11:9----------114
12:7-----------33

John
1:5------------80
4:14-----------76
8:12-----------80
14:15----------62
14:20----------80
14:26---------154

II Corinthians
5:10-----------62
5:21-----------57

Galatians
5:22,23---124,190

Titus
1:2-----------113

Hebrews
13:2----------187

James
4:2-----------114

Revelation
4:8------------87
13:15---------175
14:9-12-------176
21:21----------87

General Index

B

baptized 165
beast (mark of) 175, 176
bedrock 55, 59, 120
benches, stone 42
birdies 48-50, 101
bowl
    grass bowl 70, 71
    inside small cave 74
breast cancer 111-115
breath 38, 51, 52, 67, 106, 143,
       160, 166, 170, 184
bridge (golden) 83, 84
buzz (Holy Spirit) *xvi*, 148

C

cache of jewelry 31
calleth them (stars) 67
camper trailer 44, 101
cancer 106, 112, 138
    breast 111-115
    cancer-causing water 25
    chemotherapy, radiation 111
    dendritic cell therapy 111
    pathology report 111
canyon 82-84
cards (video) 57, 58, 105, 186
carried by an angel 131
cash-only property 30
catalysts 166
cataract surgery 110
cave (Owin Spring) 74, 75
cells 111, 150, 180, 184
chalices (silver) 122
chanting 87-91
chastised 33, 66, 184
check-your-card 130
cheeks 99, 129, 149

chest 52, 54, 131, 168
    chin lowered 50
    hand on (me?) 128
    weight of bricks 33
chosen one *vii*, 79
Christ (see also: Jesus Our Lord)
Christians *xv*, 36, 42, 59, 60, 104
claimed promises 112-114
closer 89, 103, 130, 188
closure allowed 147
clouds 65, 71, 72, 77, 101, 103, 115, 159
    clouds of angels 55
    going to heaven 66
    portal rim 134
    power of God 71
collapsed roof 43
collapsed tumor 113
commandments (see: Ten
    Commandments)
commendation 31
compassion 53, 57, 64, 109,
    150, 169, 170
concentrated reservoirs
    of poisons 183
crisscrossed angels sandals 87, 97
crucial message (universe) 173
cup, stone-carved 74
cures (miraculous) 106-115, 165
cyclone fence (pat-down) 127

D

darkly colored basalt 74
death decree 175
decay 177
decorative leather skirt 97
dendritic cell therapy 111
dense (veil) 157
depicted hell scenarios 174
design (gold filigree) 88, 119

Q

R

S

T